GROWING UP ON A FARM

to you with best wishes—
Donald F. Megnin

GROWING UP ON A FARM

DONALD F. MEGNIN

Copyright © 2018 by Donald F. Megnin.

Library of Congress Control Number:		2018906305
ISBN:	Hardcover	978-1-9845-3110-0
	Softcover	978-1-9845-3109-4
	eBook	978-1-9845-3108-7

All rights reserved. No part of this book may be reproduced or transmitted in any form or by any means, electronic or mechanical, including photocopying, recording, or by any information storage and retrieval system, without permission in writing from the copyright owner.

Any people depicted in stock imagery provided by Getty Images are models, and such images are being used for illustrative purposes only.
Certain stock imagery © Getty Images.

Print information available on the last page.

Rev. date: 07/20/2018

To order additional copies of this book, contact:
Xlibris
1-888-795-4274
www.Xlibris.com
Orders@Xlibris.com
777872

Growing Up On A Farm

Since I was not part of the family that first started out from Germany during the nineteen twenties, permit me to introduce the Megnin family which arrived in New York City aboard a German passenger liner on July 18, 1927. The new arrivals were my father, Frederich Eugen Megnin, my mother, Emilie Bartholomae Megnin, Volkmar Ulrich Megnin, my brother, and Ingetraude Megnin, my sister. It was a planned arrival in that my uncle, Karl Gottlieb Megnin, my father's brother, had driven to New York harbor to pick up his brother, sister-in-law, nephew and niece to drive them to Syracuse, New York where not only Karl, his wife, Anne, and son, Billy lived, but Pop's sister, Margaret Hausmann, her husband, Richard, and son Richard and daughter, Grete, also lived. It was a long drive in those days, but one which usually started out in the darkness of the early morning hours and ended after six hours later on the pier next to the ship which had brought the new comers to the United States. After the greeting between Frederick, Emilie, Volkmar, Inge and Karl had taken place, Karl went about finding the baggage which his brother and family had brought to America. After making sure all of the baggage which Karl picked out was, indeed, from his brother's family, he loaded it into his car and made sure the rest would be shipped to 410 Delmar Place in Syracuse, New York.

After making sure that everything had been accounted for and was addressed to Karl's Syracuse address, Karl took them to his car and had them pile into it for the long drive back to Syracuse. They stopped after a few hours at a restaurant and had lunch before continuing their long trip. Emilie was still not very lively since she

DONALD F. MEGNIN

had been very seasick for most of the trip across the ocean. With a few cups of coffee and lunch, she gradually became more responsive as the drive continued to Syracuse. Pop was pleased with how well Volkmar and Inge took to the ship travel. Neither of them had become seasick during the entire trip in contrast to their mother. Upon their arrival in Syracuse, Karl put them up in his new house in Lyncourt which was only partially completed. At least they had a comfortable place to stay and slept long hours into the next day.

By lunch time, Karl had taken them to the house which Richard Hausmann had found available for them not far from where he lived on Knaul Street. While Pop thought the house was too small for them. Richard told him

"Es gibt Hauser in die neue tel die Du selber sehen kannst, Friederich. Ihr müssen nicht lang hier bleiben." ("There are a lot of houses available here, Frederick. You won't have to stay here very long.")

"Ja, das werde ich tun." ("Yes, that's what I'll be doing.")

It was a joyous reunion between Emilie, Gretel and Grossmutter Megnin. Grossmutter had come to America with the Hausmanns and had written very favorable letters to Pop and Mom describing how much they liked their move to America.

"Es gibt viele Geschaefft in America, Frederich. Du wirst so fort eine Stelle finden was Dir gefalt!"

("There is a lot business in America. You won't have any problem finding a job, Frederich.")

One of the first things Frederich did was look for a bigger house to rent. He was still used to the large house he had owned in Germany which comprised not only his own residence, but his workshop as well. He eventually found a large house on North Salina Street next to the elementary school in which to enroll Volkmar and Inge in the appropriate grades. Gretel was a big help to him and helped enroll his children in the appropriate classes consistent with what they had experienced in Germany. Karl and Richard took Frederick to the Easy Washer Company and he was immediately hired as a tool maker. Fortunately, Karl was readily available as a translator as it might become necessary to interpret for Frederick what he was expected to do in his new job. He was also enrolled in the night school where he and Emilie learned to speak, read and write English as their newest language. One of the earliest frustrations for Frederick, however, was an inability to communicate with Americans due to his inability to speak loudly enough to be understood in his new language due to his wartime injury from World War I. The frustration continued to develop even after he had had a few different jobs. The people whom he encountered continued to say they couldn't understand what he was saying. He wasn't speaking loudly enough!

It was after this final job that he had encountered so much difficulty in having Americans understand him (he opened a car repair shop in one of the Syracuse districts) that he simply was never understood by his customers who would say

"Fred, can your wife speak English?" When he said yes, they would ask him "Go get your wife. I'll tell her what I need!"

These daily interrogations were simply more than he could bear! He decided he would look for a farm in the Syracuse area in which he wouldn't have to interact with anyone who claimed they couldn't understand what he was saying! Hence, he found the farm of his choice at R.D.#1, Chittenango, New York 13037 which he bought for twenty thousand dollars in December of 1928.

The Earliest Days on the Farm

When we arrived on the farm in January, 1929 (I was born on December 10, 1928), the farm buildings consisted of the house, built in 1793, the horse barn, on the eastern part of the yard, the well, to the southeast slightly behind our garage, and the garden, to the south and west of the house, set off in a large yard with pear trees, plum trees, grapes and lilac bushes on the front of the garden near the highway. There was also one of the largest elm trees we had ever seen growing on the eastern end of the house between the sidewalk and the driveway spreading its limbs towards the south, the west (over the front end of the house), and over the highway to the north. There were no longer any branches extending from the elm tree towards the east due to the fact that the limbs had broken off years before and the opening had been covered by concrete spread over the space where the eastern limbs had broken off. The stump of the tree was more than thirty feet in diameter. It was by far the largest tree we had ever seen except for a few still remaining in our northern woodlot.

The horse barn was for the horses that pulled the stage coach along the highway in the previous century and they were kept overnight in the basement of the barn separated from the basement floor by a three inch thick ceiling keeping the hay for the horses above them. The water for the horses was kept in the twenty-two foot deep well just to the east of the garage. While the water was hauled to the water tank daily from the water pumped from the well, it eventually was fenced off just to the south of the pump where the water was then pumped directly into tubs placed inside the barnyard fence which kept the cows and horses in the extended barnyard and pasture beyond the pump where the water was then pumped directly into tubs placed inside the barnyard fence which kept the cows and horses in the extended barnyard and pasture on the nearby fields and hills.

The barns across the highway (on the north side of the highway) were huge by local standards. There was a huge horse barn, workshop, and storage area just across the street from the western end of the house. This is where the horses were housed over the winters. There were two blind horses, (Dick and Lady) black and white on their faces and a gray horse (Tom) which could see and each time my father wanted to catch him in the yard, he would run away and could only be caught when he ended up in the area between the rail fences which circumnavigated the entire farm and the fields in between. My father eventually decided to tie him to a wagon wheel with a rope and which the horse (Tom) pulled around from pasture to pasture and water stream to drink as he wished. At least he could be caught when he was needed to work on the farm. The other two horses (Dick and Lady) wandered from field to field as well as they could since they were both blind, but able to find the ponds or streams to quench their thirst as best as they could. While Tom was by far the strongest horse on the farm, trying to catch him simply became too onerous and, therefore, Pop simply tied him to a wagon wheel which he dragged around while eating whatever grass he could find to his satisfaction.

The horse barn was ideal for the horses. Tom had his own stall to which he was tied daily during the winter and only taken out to pull the manure wagon each morning to one of the fields where Pop spread the manure. He only used Dick and Lady when he wanted to make sure they would be most useful and helpful when he took his older son along with him to spread the manure. Tom had a tendency to want to keep moving rather than wait until the manure from the cow barn had been spread by pitch fork.

The horse barn was divided into three separate sections. On the western end, the horses were tethered to the walls from which they ate their hay and occasional grain. There was actually room for four horses along the rear wall but since Pop only had three there was one space in which he kept his grain which he occasionally fed his horses.

In the winter, he led the horses out to the well on the eastern end of the barn yard to let them drink from the tank which he pumped full each time he had either his horses or his cows out in the barnyard. He had to tie Tom to the well shed so that he wouldn't try to run away and he had to lead him back to the horse barn and tie him into his stall each time Tom had had enough to drink. Dick and Lady weren't a problem. They simply stood and waited until Pop led them to the water tank which he had pumped full for them to drink.

Just behind the area in which the horses were tethered, was a work shop in which Pop could work to repair his equipment or tinker with his machinery to run more smoothly. Just beyond his workshop there was an outdoor wagon cover under which Pop could store his hay in the event of a rain storm or simply to store his wagons to keep them dry when not in use.

The really big barn was the cow barn in which he had fifteen cows which he and Mom milked by hand each morning and evening. The barn was built facing east and west so that the cows were in the barn yard to the south of the barn when they went outside of the barn to drink water from the tank next to the well on the north side of the road next to the highway. I still remember sitting on a stool between the two rows of cows being milked by my parents while watching them as they moved from cow to cow. On one occasion Mom was so sleepy she sat down next to the bull at the end of the row of cows on the right side and Pop walked up to her and laughed "You're not going to get much milk out of him!"

On the eastern end of the barn sat the largest silo in Onondaga County, we were told by the salesman who sold the farm to Pop. It towered over the barns and the base of the silo is still recognizable even today (October 5, 2017) from the concrete which was poured shortly after the beginning of the 20th century. The silo filling took place with the help of our neighbors who then also had the help of Pop. It was the custom of those days that each farmer helped his neighbors and they then helped them in doing the same. Since Pop didn't have a corn harvester, he depended upon his neighbors to cut the corn into bundles which were then picked up by the horses and wagons as the farmers pitched the bundled corn on the wagons to haul to the silo filler at the silo where it was then thrown into the filler which chopped up the corn which was then blown into the silo for winter storage and distribution each day during the winter season. My older brother, Volkmar, had the job of throwing down the ensilage to the base of the silo in the cow barn where Pop then distributed the chopped up corn to the cows as they stood in stanchions and waited for the chopped up corn. I used to sit on one of the milk stools on the platform where the ensilage was thrown down while Pop and Mom milked the cows. As they moved down the line of cows to milk, I would move my stool along the center of the barn between the two sides of the gutters to watch as they milked the cows. In contrast to the cow barns which we built later, the center corridor was made of wood as were the gutters and the areas where the cows stood and slept. The aisles leading into and out of the cow barn were also all made of wood.

As we looked over the remnants of the barns since the era of the 18th century in which these old barns were built, concrete has replaced the wood not only where the cows stood and slept, but in the aisles leading into and out of the cow barns. One additional feature which I found later to be rather unique about this old wooden cow barn was the huge door leading out to the north of the barn and looking down into a low spot in the field just below the cow barn. The opening had a large door which was open occasionally on hot days and which was used to throw out the manure from the gutters until a large pile of manure had accumulated which was then loaded into the manure wagons and taken out to the fields to be distributed as fertilizer. I remember one day when my parents had completed milking the cows, Pop was driving them out of the barn when one of the cows turned towards the open door and jumped out into the manure pile some feet beneath where she landed. It took her some time to gradually retrieve her feet so that she could walk off the pile unto solid ground again! Pop never left the door open after that until the cows had all left the barn through the regular entrance into the barn yard!

DONALD F. MEGNIN

I should also mention it was just in the previous December 10, 1928, that I was born in Syracuse, New York in a Catholic Women's Hospital on Grand Boulevard. My father had already decided he had had enough of the different attempts to find jobs that were of interest to him and in which he had to be understood by the employers. The purchase of a farm was totally new to him. He had never even visited a farm in Germany in all of the years that he lived there. He literally had no idea how to work on a farm or even how to milk a cow! Fortunately for him, he had a neighbor, Frank May, who lived just two farms to the west of him on route five who also had a problem with his speaking capabilities and took in interest in this new neighbor. He literally became his teacher, neighbor and friend who taught him how to care for his cows, horses, and what crops to raise and how to prepare each of his fields for the various types of crops he would have to raise for his animals. One of the hardest but most important jobs which he taught him was how to milk his newly purchased cows!

Fortunately for Frederick and Emily, Frank May had observed Richard driving the wagon with the horses, tools, and equipment on the wagon from Manlius and had then followed him to the farm to introduce himself and help Frederick and Richard put the horses into their proper barn and then help to put the cows into the cow barn. They had been brought to the farm that same day so that Frank was helpful in not only putting the cows into the stanchions, but also to help them milk the cows that first night. He then had to go home and milk his own cows that same evening. It was the start of a training program which was of enormous help to Frederick and Richard for their initial introduction to farming which they only recognized years later had begun with this initial introduction to farming which they only recognized years later had begun with this initial introduction of their neighbor by his helpfulness. Fortunately for Pop and Mom, my arrival had helped the Hausmanns to decide to come to the farm to help in doing the necessary work which could only be done by them since Mom was so busy taking care of me as the newly arrived Megnin baby!

It also meant that Uncle Richard and Aunt Margaret had decided to move into the larger of the two houses on the farm in order to establish a tourist home for travelers using the New York Route 5 state highway as their major means to travel eastward to Albany, New York City, and New England or to Rochester, Buffalo, or westward to other western cities. It was the start of an adventure which none of them had had any idea would occur. It also meant that Grete, the younger daughter of the Hausmanns would walk each morning to the Mycenae School House with Volkmar and Inge to attend school. The Hausmann's son, Richard, had entered the College of Forestry in Syracuse and, subsequently, remained in their house in Syracuse, New York.

That first summer was an exceptional introduction to farming for Frederick Megnin and Richard Hausmann, since neither of them had ever farmed nor were familiar with farming, had it not been for Frank May, their experiences in learning how to farm could have been disastrous! Frank seemed to check on them almost daily to make sure they were doing the right things with the cows, horses and crops in the fields.

The farm consisted of three large farm buildings on the opposite sides of the road from the farm house. On the extreme westside was the horse barn, a large building capable of housing four horses with their own hay barn just over head and ample room for wagons to keep under the roof on the eastern end of the barn. Since Pop only had three horses, he had room to store his grain and tools in the empty space reserved for the fourth horse. The horse barn was just across the road from the western end of the house. The cow barn was the next barn just to the east of the horse barn. Here Pop had stanchioned his fifteen cows facing north and south inside the barn with the gutters flowing east and west in their wooden troughs with the largest silo in the county abutting the east and west in their wooden troughs with the largest silo in the county abutting the eastern end of the barn. As a little boy, it was my privilege to sit on a stool just where the silage was thrown down from the silo during the milking period and then periodically I'd move my stool along the central runway as

DONALD F. MEGNIN

my parents moved from cow to cow to milk them. I was too young to attend the milking session of Pop and Uncle Richard, but I did so of Mom and Pop after the Hausmanns returned to their home at 207 Knaul Street in Syracuse, New York.

One of the first tragedies that we experienced on the farm was the fire which started in the horse barn hay mow. It was late in the afternoon of July 1932, that Volkmar came running into the cow barn as Mom and Pop were milking the cows.

"Pop!" Volkmar yelled out as he came into the cow barn. "The horse barn is on fire! Should I let the horses out?"

"Ja, sicher! Und dann geh hinunter zum Benzine stelle und frag der Geschaettsman er sol die Firewehr anrufen und sagen einen von unseren Schonen ist im flammen!"

("Yes, indeed! And then go down to the gas station and have them call the Chittenenago Fire Department and tell them one of our barns is on fire!")

Volkmar did as he was told and then came into the cow barn again to help Pop drive out the cows from the barn before it too caught fire! Volkmar drove the cows and horses out into the nearby pasture. The Chittenango Fire Department finally arrived as did the Kirkville and Minoa Fire Departments to try to control the fire from spreading across the street to the house. The house was saturated with water so that it literally steamed. The Minoa Fire Department kept spraying the house and also the well shed on the north side of Route 5 since it was so close to the burning barn and silo. The constant showering of the well shed kept it from bursting into flames as the other buildings had done from one barn to the next. It did mean Pop was able to keep the water tank as a useful addition across the road in the rear of the building which he built over the well.

The upshot of the total burning of all of the buildings on the north side of the highway was that Mr. Nesbitt told Pop,

"Fred, you can put your cows into my barn since its empty! There's plenty of hay and ensilage in my barn and silo so you shouldn't have any problems feeding your cows as much as they need. Subsequently, Pop and the neighbors drove the cows up to the Nesbitt farm and installed them in an abundant location with plenty of food and water for the cows. It was only close to a month later that Pop asked Mr. Nesbitt, "What are you going to charge me for boarding my cows and calves with you, Mr. Nesbitt? They are eating heavily from your hay and ensilage."

"Oh I guess maybe two or three dollars a day should be plenty. Don't worry about it, Fred. There's plenty of time before spring comes around and the cows will be back out on pasture."

Pop thanked Mr. Nesbitt and then decided at that rate of repayment, he would soon run out of money. He arranged with his brother, Karl, to visit the auctioneer in Manlius from whom he purchased the cows to arrange a time for an auction to sell his cows and young stock as soon as possible. It was that next week that the auction took place and Frederick sold all but three of his cows and calves ranging from sixty dollars per cow to ten to fifteen dollars per calf at the auction. He kept his favorite Holstein heifer and his all black Holstein cow, and another spotted Holstein in order to rebuild his dairy after he had rebuilt another cow barn adjacent to the hay barn which he still had on the same side of the road as the house. It was then that he took Tom and Dick down to the Schlucht (valley) each day to cut down Hemlock trees which he then had them pull up to the field just behind where the cow barn had stood. It was here that he decided would be the best place for a sawmill to be set up to cut the trees into boards, two-by-fours, two-by-sixes, two-by-eights and two-by-twelves for the building of a new barn next to the hay barn which still existed next to the house on the south side of Route Five. It was that next year that Pop hired a sawmill owner to come to the farm and saw up his collection of logs which he had gathered behind where the cow barn had originally stood. He had also hired Carly Leach, who lived in Mycenae, to work with him not only to saw up the logs which Pop had cut, but also to help him rebuild a cow barn so that he could once again have a monthly milk check to deposit in the Chittenango State Bank.

Overall, Frederick was pleased with the progress he was making in rebuilding his barn and anticipating once again to have a supply of milk to send to the Queensborough Milk Company. Fortunately, for Frederick, he had made enough from the sale of his cows, at the auction to be able to hire Carly and begin rebuilding his new cow barn. They worked together in digging out the base of his new cow barn walls to a depth of three feet and to a height of five feet and the wall on the eastern end and southern sides of the new barn. The northern side was just four feet high including the first three feet in the ground.

It should be noted, the fire which started in the horse barn, simple continued to ignite not only the cow barn, but then also the silo. When Pop asked why the firemen were not hosing the cow barn after the fire burned out in the horse barn, their answer was

"We really can't contain the fire on the north side of the road. The only thing we can do is try to prevent it from spreading across the road and set your house on fire! It looks like what we are doing is going to work. Your house is only steaming. It's not burning anywhere, Mr. Megnin."

And with that explanation, the firemen from Chittenango and Kirkville kept their hoses trained on wetting down the house from the front to the rear. It never caught fire.

It should be noted that by September, 1929, the Hausmanns were already through with their interest in sharing the work on the farm with Mom and Pop. The Hausmanns had decided the tourist business without indoor toilets and bathrooms was not for them. They told Pop and Mom that they were going back to the city and said the big old house was theirs to use and they could rent out the small house in which they had been living. Needless to say, Pop and Mom were greatly disappointed but, since they had no other option, accepted the Hausmanns departure with some degree of anger and disappointment!

It should be noted that Grete, the Hausmann's teenage daughter who had been attending the local grade school in Mycenae with Volkmar and Inge, was now withdrawn from that school and enrolled in a grade school near Knaul Street where the Hausmanns lived. Volkmar and Inge had to walk back and forth from the Mycenae school to the farm alone since Pop had no car in which to take them back and forth. Previously, Volkmar and Inge were accompanied by Grete and now they were once again alone.

Since this was the time of the Great Depression of the 1930s, not only Pop and Mom received very little money for the milk they were producing, but generally all farm products were selling at a very minimum price! There were men on the street every day seeking something to eat from Mom and asking if they might have something to do to pay back the cost of the food which they were consuming. Invariably Mom turned them down and simply gave them a sandwich and an apple or a piece of pie, if she had made one. They were very thankful and Mom told us not to stand around while they were eating because they would usually ask for another sandwich or piece of cake if one of us was standing around watching them eat their lunch. Another of the privileges which the men often asked was

"Can I spend the night in your hayloft until morning and then I'll be on my way?"

Pop usually allowed then the privilege to do so with the caution, "There's no smoking allowed in the hay barn!"

"Oh don't worry about that! I don't even have any money to buy cigarettes!"

And usually, Pop allowed them to climb up into the haymow to spend the night sleeping in the hay loft!

Unfortunately, Frank May warned Frederick about making sure the hay was dry before he put it in the hayloft, only to have Frederick decide it was close to dry when he put a damp load of alfalfa and timothy into the horse barn hayloft only to have it heated up and ignite while they were milking the cows on the evening of July 1932. Volkmar was the first to discover the smoke coming out of the horse barn hay loft and he ran back to the cow barn to alert Pop and Mom.

"Pop, there's smoke coming out of the horse barn! Should I let the horses out?"

"Ja! Und dann renn zum Auto Geschaft und sag Ihnen wir haben einen Fire Anfang im unseren Pferde Schoane!"

DONALD F. MEGNIN

("Yes! And then go to the gas station and call the fire department that we have a fire in our horse barn!")

Volkmar ran as fast as he could and the gas station owner called the Chittenango Fire Department which came immediately. They turned their hoses on the house first of all since the buildings were just across the street and the house immediately began to receive a stream of cold water on the roof and sides of the house. They then turned the hoses on the horse barn and then the cow barn since the wind was blowing in an easterly direction. Volkmar had let the horses out of the horse barn and had driven them down the road way towards the lower fields. He then headed for the cow barn in which Pop and Mom were already letting the cows and calves out and driving them down into the nearby fields away from the fires which were now breaking out in the cow barn and silo. Pop was disappointed with the activities of the Chittenango firemen since they were directing their hoses on the house and milk shed across the road. Pop could not understand why the firemen were directing so much effort on these further removed buildings while the fire was consuming the barns and silo!

"Why aren't you directing your hoses on the horse barn and the cow barn?" He yelled as loudly as he could!

"Because those two buildings are already in flames and I don't think it's going to do any good to waste water on them anymore! I've called the Fayetteville and Minoa fire departments to come and help us. We don't want your house to catch fire, too!"

Needless to say, not only the horse barn, cow barn and silo were consumed by the flames, but there was nothing left of the equipment which had also been inside the tool shed next to the horse barn. By the time the other two fire departments arrived, it was too late to do more than keep the water pouring on the house across the street to make sure it would not catch fire!

Pop was at a loss to know what to do next. He had a barn across the road, but it was not prepared for the number of cows he had nor where he night put his horses. As he was considering what he was going to do next, his neighbor from across the road some distance away found him and suggested, "Fred, why don't you put your cows in my barn? I've sold all of my cows and the barn and silo are filled with food that the cows would enjoy eating."

"Thanks, Mr. Nesbitt. That would be a big help for me right now. There's nothing left to house them here anymore!"

And with these words, the Nesbitts and neighbors, who had been watching the fires, rounded up the cattle and drove them along the highway up to the Nesbitt farm along with the three horses. It wasn't very far, less than half a mile towards Chittenango. The cows felt right at home eating the ensilage and hay from the Nestbitt's barn and silo. Pop and Mom finished milking the cows and returned to the house in time for Mom to make supper for the family. Pop took two of the horses back to the house where he put his milk cans in the cold water of the cooling tank near where the fire had burned off the rest of the buildings. A neighbor had brought the milk cans to the Nesbitt barn where Pop poured the milk as they completed milking the cows. He then put the three horses in the shed behind the hay barn next to the house in what then became the barnyard next to the house.

Each morning, Pop and Mom rode up to the Nesbitt barn in the wagon drawn by Dick and Tom to milk the cows and feed and water them before taking the milk back to the milk house where the delivery truck stopped each morning to pick up the milk cans to take them to the Chittenango Milk Factory. After a week of this arrangement, Pop asked Mr. Nesbitt what he was going to charge him for the use of his barn and feeding his cows and horses?

"It won't be too much, Fred. I think maybe two to three dollars a day should pretty much cover the costs for the use of my barn and feeding your animals."

Pop thanked him for the information and said he was going to have his animals auctioned off as soon as he could because he could no longer afford the cost of boarding them in the Nesbitt barn. Since Pop had bought an old Willys-Knight, he drove it over to his brother's house that evening and talked with him about contacting an auctioneer to schedule an early date to sell his cows.

DONALD F. MEGNIN

"I certainly can't afford to keep the cows much longer in the Nesbitt barn, Karl. It's already cost me more than thirty dollars and if this goes on much longer, I won't have any money left!"

"I'll go with you, Fritz, to talk with the man whose an auctioneer in Jamesville. He's the same one you bought your cows, machinery, and equipment from when you first started farming."

"Okay Karl. That would be a big help. We'll visit him this next Saturday when you're free from your job at the Easy Washer."

On that next Saturday morning, Karl arrived at eight o'clock to drive Pop up to the auctioneer's house to discuss setting up a date for the sale of his eighteen cows so that he could pay Mr. Nesbitt for the use of his barn, hay, ensilage and water for his cows after the fire. The auction was held that next Saturday at nine o'clock in the barn of the Nesbitt's farm. There were many farmers in attendance even though the advertisement was mostly by word of mouth. The neighbors had alerted the community about the auction and while it was only for the sale of fifteen cows and a couple of caves, the response from the community was impressive. Pop got an average of sixty dollars per cow (Holsteins) so that he could pay Mr. Nesbitt for the cost of the hay and ensilage, but charged nothing for the use of his barn. Pop offered to pay him rent but Mr. Nesbitt said, "Don't worry about it, Fred. I've got more than enough manure to make up for any rental cost for the use of the barn!" he said as he laughed at his own joke!

After the Sale of the Cows

Pop kept three cows from the eighteen that he originally had. Two Holsteins, a mostly black one and a mostly white one, plus the young Holstein heifer which impressed him with her growth and sharp demeanor in protecting herself when she drank at the water tanks. Even some of the older cows didn't bother to contest her access to the water tanks when they wanted to drink. They simply waited until she was through and had left the water tanks when she had enough.

One of the first jobs that Pop undertook, besides cutting down hemlock and spruce trees in our woods and hauling them up behind where the cow barn had been, was to make room for the cows under the hay in the barn near the house. He dug a long gutter across the back of the barn on the first floor which he then blocked off with wood and poured concrete in it to make the gutter permanent and erected three stanchions in which to keep the cows while being milked or over the winter months. He also made sure there was enough room for him to place hay and grain in front of the cows with stanchions to make sure they would remain here for longer periods of time as it might become necessary. He placed the horses in the covered shanty which he had attached to the rear of the hay barn and made an area out of which they could eat the hay which he placed in front of them and the occasional oats or grain he gave them as his money permitted. It was from this lean to shed behind the barn which had been used to tether the horses pulling the stagecoaches in the nineteenth and early twentieth centuries along Route Five, which became the shed in which the horses were kept each year when not on pasture. He took Dick and Tom down to the woods and began to cut down hemlock, spruce, ash and maple trees into twelve foot length logs which he had the two horses pull up into the field just behind where the cow barn had stood. After amassing more than two hundred of these logs, he hired a sawmill owner to bring his sawmill over to the field of logs and set it up to saw the logs into two by twelves, two by tens, two by fours and inch boards with which to construct a new barn for his next herd of cows. As I mentioned earlier, he had hired Carly Leach, from Mycenae, to come to the farm to work with him and especially to help him build his new barn on the east side of the hay barn to the southeast of the farm where we lived.

Since Pop had closed down the gas station and the pumps had been removed, the rock cutter along Chittenango Creek up towards Chittenango Falls, stopped and talked to Pop about renting the gas station shed and the nearby lot in order to sell his beautiful rocks which he had dug out of the creek and creekside hills below the falls. Pop thought this was an excellent idea and agreed to rent his building and local grounds for him to set up his displays. He did an excellent job displaying his deeply etched rocks not only in the office space, but in the nearby yard. Mom had planted a ring of flowers near where the cars had stopped to have their gas tanks filled from the nearby pumps. The stone cutter then proceeded to set his ring of etched rocks just outside of the ring of flowers which set them off beautifully for everyone to enjoy. The stone cutter's sons managed the business and included hosting a small ice cream and candy shop in the building from which they could oversee the rocks displayed outside on the porch and along the roadway and adjacent lot which had been our camping ground for persons who wished to park overnight on their long trips to Albany, New York City and New England.)

On one occasion, a group of gypsies pulled into the camping ground and asked if they might spend the night. Pop agreed and they set up their tents behind the rock sales displays and used our outdoor toilet facilities at the end of our garage behind the house. The Gypsies liked the area so much they asked if they could stay longer than overnight. They were willing to pay the nightly fee and after a few days some of the ladies asked Mom if they could use her sewing machine to mend some of their clothes. She allowed them to do so with the proviso that they do their sewing on the porch behind the house. This system worked for a few days when they asked if Mom had any extra thread and patches they could use to mend their torn clothing. Mom had also noticed that the Gypsy children were going into our garden behind the house and helping themselves to the fruits and vegetables which were growing so well in our garden. Needless to say, Mom was upset by this taking off with her fruits and vegetables from her garden and told Pop about it. He said he would talk to the Gypsy leader, which he did. It was in this time frame that the sons of the stone cutter complained that some of the Gypsy children were taking candy off their counters and not paying for them. Pop talked to the Gypsy leader and warned "If you don't keep your children out of our garden and if they don't pay for the candy that they take from the boys in the stone shop, then you're going to have to leave!"

"I'll talk to the parents," Chief said, "We like your place here and we'd like to stay longer."

The Chief talked to the parents about the thievery from the garden and the rocks, but it continued. The Stone Cutter told Pop he was losing too much money to theft to make it worth his while to rent the display space from him.

"If their thievery doesn't stop, I'll have to call it quits, Fred!"

Pop went over to the Chief and said, "I've had enough complaints from my wife and stone cutter about what your boys are doing to her garden and their business! I want you to leave this afternoon or I'm calling the State Police and have you evicted. I can't have all of this stealing going on for which nothing is paid!"

"Okay, Fred. I'll tell my friends we'll to leave. We've enjoyed being here very much. You've got a really nice place for campers, but it you want us to leave, then we'll have to go!"

The Chief then went to each of the tents and told the guests to pack up their things and take down their tents. "Fred doesn't want us here any longer!"

Within an hour the Gypsies had taken down their tents, packed up their cars, and had driven off towards Chittenango and eastward.

The Yearly Megnin Event

One of the earliest occasions that I can remember of having all of our relatives on the farm was over the Fourth of July, 1935. It was the annual meeting for the 4th of July picnic which the Frederick Megnin family hosted each year for relatives and friends to celebrate this annual holiday which pleased everyone who attended. The relatives and friends included the Karl Megnins (Karl, Anne and Billie), the Hausmanns (Richard, Gretel, plus Dick, Grete, Billie and Susan Weiss), Klumps, (Karl, Sophie and Hilde), the Dietzes (Karl, Sophie and Richard). Mister Nicke (Tante Eliese and Wally), plus our family: Pop, Mom, Volkmar, Inge and Fritzle (Donald). There were tables and chairs set up in the camping ground under the large elm tree plus the beer barrel and wine bottles so that no one was left with nothing to drink should their glasses become empty!

The Intrigue of a Young Boy for Swallows

The garage was behind the house, but attached to the house and had a wide open end which looked out over the garden and hillside. As a seven year old, I was fascinated by the fact that swallows were building a nest on one of the beams holding up the roof. They kept flying in and out of the garage and were beginning to build a nest near the top of the inside of the garage just under the roof. I watched this activity very closely and was impressed with the fact that it didn't seem to matter to the swallows that I was watching their efforts without trepidation. After a week of watching this activity, I noticed that one of the swallows kept sitting in the nest. I wondered what it was doing so I went out to the pump house and got the long connected pole which Pop used to fish out items that had fallen into the well on occasion. It was just long enough for me to reach the nest in which the swallow was sitting. I poked around the outside of the nest and the swallow flew out and sounded the alarm which drew her mate into the garage and together they kept flying around from the nest to the ceiling of the back of the garage and then inside again. After some effort, I had been able to reach the nest with the hook on the end of the pole which caught the edge of the nest and I pulled down on it spilling out the eggs and tearing open the side of the nest. Needless to say, the swallows set up an uproar of activity making noise and flying in and out of the garage so often that Mom came down from the garden to see what was wrong in the garage. When she saw me and the swallow's nest on the floor of the garage and saw the birds flying back and forth she looked at me as I was still holding the pole and asked,

DONALD F. MEGNIN

"Donald, was hast Du getan zu diesen Swalben Nest? Weshalb ist es am Boden?" ("Donald, what did you do to the swallow's nest? Why is it on the ground?")

"I wanted to see what they would do if I put a pole up to their nest."

"Und was hast Du gelearnt von diesen Probe?" ("And what have you learned from this test?")

("I didn't think the nest would fall down so quickly.")

"Und yetzt haben die Swalben keinen Nest mer! Die Eier sind überall am Boden und es wird keinen Swalben geben diseses Jahr! Das kannst Du nicht tun! Die Swalben koenen keine Yungen haben dieses Jahr. Es ist wirklich schade was Du getan hast!" "And the swallows don't have a nest anymore. The eggs are all over the ground and there won't be any young swallows this year! It's really too bad what yo've done!")

The Purchase of Goats

In the mid-thirties, Pop decided to buy some goats. He thought if he sold goats' milk he would have a more expensive product and receive more per quart than from cows' milk. He wrote letters to the various hospitals in Syracuse only to have them write back "We would be glad to receive such a supply of goats' milk, but you would have to deliver it daily to our hospital."

Since Pop had neither a truck nor a car large enough to convey the milk to the hospitals, there was no way he could deliver the goats' milk even if the hospitals were willing to purchase it. Needless to say, he wasn't going to buy a truck for this occasion (he could not afford one), so he simply let his calves drink the milk from the goats themselves! He built a milk stand upon which the goats were kept in a stanchion while the calves sucked the milk from the goats. It worked well for the calves, but the goats suffered through the repeated head butts of the calves trying to draw more milk from the goats after they had finished their attempts to retrieve more milk after they had drained the goats!

After Pop and Carly Leach had completed building the new cow barn adjacent to the hay barn on the east side of the barn, Pop decided it might be a better idea to milk the cows on the north side of Route Five rather than have to drive the cows across the road twice a day and take chances on whether or not the large trucks could stop in time for the cows were crossing the highway. He did have a few instances where some very large trucks had been unable to stop in time and had run into a couple of cows that were ambling across the highway each evening. Invariably, the cows had to be sold to one of the butchers who drove by each day and stopped to find out if Pop had a cow or a bull calf to sell from his herd. If the cow had died before the butcher stopped to enquire if he had any cows or calves to sell, the butcher would buy the cow and put her into his truck to take her to the slaughter house to complete the slaughter and drain the insides while hanging up the rest of the carcass to cut into various sizes he wished to sell to the nearby butcher and meat shops.

As I've already indicated, when Pop bought the goats, he thought they would be an asset to the local hospitals in Syracuse for patients having a need for a higher caliber of milk as part of their diet. When he wrote the hospitals indicating he had goats milk available for patients, they immediately wrote back and indicted they would be pleased to have him ship a daily supply, however, they were not in a position to have the milk picked up and shipped to their hospitals! He would have to make these arrangements himself. Since he had neither a car large enough to do so, nor a truck to make such deliveries, he was left with his only option as I've mentioned "giving the milk to his calves, cats and dogs!

Early Days on the Farm

When we arrived on the farm in January 1929, the farm buildings consisted of the house, built in 1793, the horse barn, on the easter part of the yard, the well, to the southeast slightly behind our garage, and the garden, to the south and west of the house, set off in a large yard with pear trees, plum trees, grapes and lilac bushes to the front of the garden near the highway. There was also a large thorn bush just outside of the living room window towards the western end of the house. There were also chestnut trees just in front of the house. A rain catcher covered the porch on the front of the house. There was also one of the largest elm trees we had ever seen growing on the eastern end of the house between the sidewalk and the driveway spreading its limbs towards the south, the west (over the front end of the house), and over the highway to the north. There were no longer any branches extending from the elm tree towards the east due to the fact that the limbs had broken off years before and the opening had been covered by concrete spread over the space where the eastern limbs had broken off. The stump of the tree was more than thirty feet in diameter. It was by far the largest tree we had ever seen except for a few still remaining in our northern woodlot.

The horse barn was for the horses that pulled the stagecoaches along the highway in the previous century and they were kept overnight in the basement of the barn separated from the basement floor by a three inch thick ceiling keeping the hay for the horses above them. The water for the horses was kept in the twenty-two foot deep well just to the eastern end of the garage. While the water was hauled to the water tank daily from the water pumped from the

DONALD F. MEGNIN

well, it eventually was fenced off just to the south of the pump where the water was then pumped directly into tubs placed inside barnyard fence which kept the cows and horses in the extended barnyard and pasture beyond the pump which was then pumped directly into tubs placed inside the barnyard fence which kept the cows and horses in the extended barnyard and pasture on the nearby fields and hills.

The barns across the highway (on the north side of the highway) were huge by local standards. There was a huge horse barn, workshop, and storage area just across the street from the western end of the house. This is where the horses were housed over the winters. There were two blind horses. (Dick and Lady) black and white on their faces and a gray horse (Tom) which could see and each time my father wanted to catch him in the yard he would run away and could only be caught when he ended up in the area between the rail fences which circumnavigated the entire farm and the fields in between. My father eventually decided to tie him to a wagon wheel with a rope and which the horse (Tom) then pulled around from pasture to pasture and water stream to drink as he wished. At least he could be caught when he was needed to work on the farm. The other two horses (Dick and Lady) wandered from field to field as well as they could since they were both blind, but able to find the ponds or stream to quench their thirst as best they could. While Tom was by far the strongest horse on the farm, trying to catch him simply became too onerous and, therefore, Pop simply tied him to a wagon wheel which he dragged around while eating whatever grass he could find to his satisfaction.

The horse barn was ideal for the horses. Tom had his own stall to which he was tied daily during the winter and only taken out to pull the manure wagon each morning to one of the fields where Pop spread the manure. He only used Dick and Lady when he wanted to make sure they would be most useful and helpful when he took his older son along with him to spread the manure. Tom had a tendency to want to keep moving rather than wait until the manure from the cow barn had been spread by pitch fork.

The horse barn was divided into three separate actions. On the western end, the horses were tethered to the walls from which they ate their hay and occasional grain. There was actually room for four horses along the rear wall but since Pop only had three there was one space in which he kept his grain which he occasionally fed his horses. In the winter, he led the horses out to the well on the eastern end of the barn yard to let them drink from the tank which he pumped full each time he had either his horses or his cows out in the barn yard. He had to tie Tom to the well shed so that he wouldn't try to run away and he had to lead him back to the horse barn and tie him into his stall each time Tom had had enough to drink. Dick and Lady weren't a problem. They simply stood and waited until Pop led them to the water tank which he had pumped full for them to drink.

Just behind the area in which the horses were tethered, was a work shop in which Pop could work to repair his equipment or tinker with his machinery to run more smoothly. Just beyond his workshop there was an outdoor wagon cover under which Pop could store his hay in the event of a rain storm or simply to store his wagons to keep them dry when not in use.

The really big barn was the cow barn in which he had fifteen cows which he and Mom milked by hand each morning and evening. The barn was built facing east and west so that the cows were in the barn yard to the south of the barn when they went out side of the barn to drink water from the tank next to the well on the north side of the road next to the highway. I still remember sitting on a stool between the two rows of cows being milked by my parents while watching them as they moved from cow to cow. On one occasion Mom was so sleepy she sat down next to the bull at the end of the row of cows on the right side and Pop walked up to her and laughed "You're not going to get much milk out of him!"

On the eastern end of the barn sat the biggest silo in Onondaga County, we were told by the salesman who sold the farm to Pop. It towered over the barns and the base of the silo is still recognizable even today (September, 2017) from the concrete which was poured shortly after the beginning of the 20th century. The silo filling took place with the help of our neighbors when they also had the help of Pop. It was the custom of those days that each farmer helped his neighbors and they then helped him in doing the same. Since Pop didn't have a corn harvester he depended upon his neighbors to cut the corn into the bundles which were then picked up by the horses and wagons as the farmers pitched the bundled corn on the wagons to haul to the silo filler at the silo and was then thrown into the filler which chopped up the corn which was then blown into the silo for winter storage and distribution each day during the winter season. My older brother. Volkmar, had the job of throwing down the ensilage to the base of the silo in the cow barn where Pop then distributed the chopped up corn to the cows as they stood in their stanchions and waited for the chopped up corn. I used to sit on one of the milk stools on the platform where the ensilage was thrown down while Pop and Mom milked the cows. As they moved down the line of cows to milk, I would move my stool along the center of the barn between the two sides of the gutters to watch as they milked the cows. In contrast to the cow barns which we built later, the center corridor was made of wood as were the gutters and the areas where the cows stood and slept. The aisles leading into and out of the cow barns were also all made of wood.

As we looked over the remnants of the barns since the era of the 18th century in which these old barns were built, concrete has replaced the wood not only where the cows stood and slept, but in the aisles leading into and out of the cow barns. One additional feature which I found to be rather unique about this old wooden cow barn was the huge door leading out to the north of the barn and looking down into a low spot in the field just below the cow barn. This opening had a large door with was open occasionally on hot days and which was used to throw out the manure from the gutters until a large pile of manure had accumulated which was then loaded into the manure wagon and taken out to the fields to be distributed for fertilizer. I remember one day when my parents had completed milking the cows, Pop was driving them out of the barn when one of the cows turned towards this open door and jumped out the door into the manure pile some feet beneath where she landed. It took her some time to gradually retrieve her feet so that she could walk off the pile unto solid ground again. Pop never left the door open after that until the cows had all left the barn through the regular entrance into the barn yard!

As I've mentioned before, it was just the previous December 10, 1928, that I was born in Syracuse, New York in the Catholic Women's Hospital on Grand Boulevard. My father had already decided he had had enough of the different attempts to find jobs that were of interest to him and in which he was understood by the employers. The purchase of a farm was totally new to him. He had never even visited a farm in Germany in all of these years of living there. He literally had no idea how to work a farm or even how to milk a cow! Fortunately for him, he had a neighbor, Frank May, who lived just two farms to the west of him on route five who also had a problem with his speaking capabilities and took an interest in this new neighbor. He literally became his teacher, neighbor and friend who taught him how to care for his cows and horses and what crops to raise and how to prepare each of his fields for the various types of crops he would have to raise for his animals. One of the hardest but most important jobs which he taught him was how to milk his newly purchased cows!

Fortunately for Frederick and Emily, Frank had observed Richard driving the wagon with the horses and tools and equipment on the wagon from Manlius and had then followed him to the farm to introduce himself and help Frederick and Richard put the horses into their proper barn and then helped to put the cows into the cow barn. They had been brought to the farm that same day so that Frank was helpful in not only putting the cows into the stanchions, but also to help them milk the cows that first night. He then had to go home and milk his own cows that same evening. It was the start of a training program which was of enormous help to Frederick and Richard for their initial introduction to farming which they only recognized years later had begun with this initial introduction of their neighbor by his helpfulness. Fortunately for Pop and Mom, my arrival had helped the Hausmanns to decide to come to the farm to help in doing the necessary work which could only be done by them since Mom was so busy taking care of me as the newly born Megnin Baby!

DONALD F. MEGNIN

It also meant that Uncle Richard and Aunt Margaret had decided to move into the larger of the two houses on the farm in order to establish a tourist home for travelers using the New York Route 5 state highway as their major means to travel eastward to Albany, New York City and New England, or to Rochester, Buffalo or westward to other western cities. It was the start of an adventure which none of them had had any idea would occur. It also meant that Grete, the younger daughter of the Hausmanns, would walk each morning to the Mycenae School House with Volkmar and Inge to attend school. The Hausmann's son, Richard, had entered the College of Forestry in Syracuse and, subsequently, remained in their house in Syracuse, New York.

That first summer was an exceptional introduction to farming for Frederick Megnin and Richard Hausmann. Since neither of them had ever farmed nor were familiar with farming, had it not been for Frank May their experiences in learning how to farm could have been disastrous. Frank seemed to check on them almost daily to make sure they were doing the right things with the cows, horses and crops in the fields.

The farm consisted of three large farm buildings on the opposite side of the road from the farm house. On the extreme west was the horse barn, a large building capable of housing four horses with their own hay barn just over head and ample room for wagons to be kept under the roof on the eastern end of the barn. Since Pop had only three horses, he had room to store his grain and tools in the empty space reserved for the fourth horse. The horse barn was just across the road from the western end of the house. The cow barn was the next barn just to the east of the horse barn. Here Pop had stanchioned his fifteen cows and calves facing north and south inside the barn with gutters flowing east and west in their wooden troughs with the largest silo in the county abutting the eastern end of the barn. As a little boy, it was my privilege to it on a stool just where the silage was thrown down from the silo during the milking period and then periodically I moved my stool along the central runway as my parents moved from cow to cow to milk them. I was too young to attend the milking sessions of Pop and Uncle Richard, but did so of Mom and Pop after the Hausmanns returned to their home at 207 Knaul Street in Syracuse, New York.

One of the first tragedies that we experienced on the farm was the fire which started in the horse barn hay mow. It was late in the afternoon of July 1932, that Volkmar came running intro the cow barn as Mom and Pop were milking the cows.

"Pop!" Volkmar yelled out as he came into the cow barn, "The horse barn is on fire! Should I let the horses out?"

"Ja, sicher! Und dann geh hinunter zum Benzine stelle und frag der Geschaeffman er sol die Firewehr anrufen und sagen einen von unseren Schonen ist im flammen!"

(Yes, indeed! And then go down to the gas station and have them call the Chittenango Fire Department and tell them one of our barns is on fire!")

Volkmar did as he was told and then came into the cow barn again to help Pop drive the cows out of the barn before the cow barn caught fire. Volkmar drove the cows and horses out into the nearby pasture. The Chittenango Fire Department finally arrived as did the Kirkville and Minoa Fire Departments to try to control the fire from spreading across the street to the house. The house was saturated with water so that it literally steamed. The Minoa Fire Department kept spraying the house and also the well shed on the north side of Route 5 since it was so close to the burning barn and silo. The constant showering of the well shed kept it from bursting into flames as the other buildings had done from one barn to the next. It did mean Pop was able to keep the water tank as a useful addition across the road in the rear of the building which he built over the well. The upshot of the total burning of all of the building on the north side of the highway was that Mr. Nesbitt told Pop

"Fred you can put your cows in my barn since its empty. There's plenty of hay and ensilage in my barn and silo so you shouldn't have any problems feeding your cows as much as they need. Subsequently, Pop and the neighbors drove the cows up to the Nesbitt farm and installed them in an abundant location with plenty of food and water

DONALD F. MEGNIN

for the cows. It was only close to a month later that Pop asked Mr. Nesbitt, "What are you going to charge me for boarding my cows and calves with you, Mr. Nesbitt? They are eating heavily from your hay and ensilage."

"Oh I guess maybe two or three dollars a day should be plenty. Don't worry about it, Fred. There's plenty of time before Spring comes around and the cows will be back out on pasture."

Pop thanked Mr. Nesbitt and then decided at that rate of repayment, he would soon run out of many. He arranged with his brother, Karl, to visit the auctioneer in Manlius from whom he had purchased his cows to arrange a time for an auction to sell his cows and young stock as soon as possible. It was that next week that the auction took place and Frederick sold all of his cow and calves ranging from sixty dollars per cow to ten to fifteen dollars per calf at the auction. He kept his favorite Holstein heifer and the all black Holstein cow, and another spotted Holstein in order to rebuild his dairy after he had rebuilt another cow barn adjacent to the hay barn which he still had on the same side as the house. It was than that he took Tom and Dick down into the Schlucht (valley) easy day to cut down the Hemlock trees which he then had them pull up to the field just behind where the cow barn had stood. It was here that he decided would be the best place for a sawmill to be set up to cut the trees into boards, two-by-fours, two by sixes, two-by-eights and two-by twelves for the building of a new barn next to the hay barn which still stood next to the house on the south side of Route Five. It was that next year that pop hired the sawmill owner to come to the farm and saw up his collection of logs which he had gathered behind where the cow barn had originally stood. He had also hired Carly Leach, who lived in Mycenae, to work with him not only to saw up the logs which Pop had cut, but also to help him rebuild a cow barn so that he could once again have a monthly milk check to deposit in the Chittenango State Bank.

Overall, Frederick was pleased with the progress he was making in rebuilding his barn and anticipating once again to have a supply of milk to send to the Queensborough Milk Company. Fortunately for Frederick, he had made enough from the sale of his cows at the auction to be able to hire Carly and begin rebuilding his new cow barn. They worked together in digging out the base of his new cow barn walls to a depth of three feet and to a height of five feet for the wall on the eastern and southern sides of the new barn. The northern end was just four feet high including the first three feet in the ground.

It should be mentioned, the fire which started in the horse barn, simple continued to ignite not only the cow barn, but then also the silo. When Pop asked the firemen who were not hosing down the cow barn after the fire broke out in the horse barn, the answer was "We really can't contain the fire on this north side of the road. The only thing we can do is try to prevent it from spreading across the road and set your house on fire! It looks like what we are doing is going to work. Your house is only steaming, it's not burning anywhere, Mr. Megnin!"

And with that explanation, the firemen from Chittenango and Kirkville kept their hoses trained on wetting down the house from the front to the rear. It never caught fire.

It should be noted that by September of 1929, the Hausmanns were already through with their interest in sharing the work on the farm with Pop and Mom. The Hausmanns had decided the tourist business without indoor toilets and bathrooms was not for them. They told Pop and Mom that they were going back to the city and said the big old house was theirs to use and they could rent out the small house in which they had been living. Needless to say, Pop and Mom were greatly disappointed but, since they had no other option, accepted the Hausmanns departure with some degree of anger and disappointment.

It should also be noted that Grete, the Hausmann's teenager who had been attending the local school in Mycenae with Volkmar and Inge was now withdrawn from that school and enrolled in a grade school near Knaul Street where the Hausmanns lived. Volkmar and Inge had to walk back and forth from the Mycenae school to the farm alone since Pop had no car in which to take them back and forth. Previously, Volkmar and Inge were accompanied by Grete and now they were once again alone.

DONALD F. MEGNIN

Since this was the time of the Great Depression of the 1930s. Not only had Fred and Emilie received very little money for the milk they were producing, but generally all farm products were selling at a very minimum price! There were men on the street everyday seeking something to eat from Mom and asking if they might have something to do to pay back the cost of the food which they were consuming. Invariably Mom turned them down and simply gave them a sandwich and an apple or a piece of pie, if she had made one. They were very thankful and Mom told us not to stand around them while they were eating because they would usually ask for another sandwich or piece of cake if one of us was standing around watching them eat their lunch. Another of the privileges which the men often asked for was "Can I spend the night in your hayloft until morning and then I'll be on my way?"

Pop usually allowed them the privilege to do so with the caution, "There's no smoking allowed in the hay barn!"

"Oh don't worry about that! I don't even have any money to buy cigarettes!" And usually, Pop allowed them to climb up in the hay mow to spend the night sleeping in the hay loft.

Unfortunately Frank May warned Frederick about making sure the hay was dry before he put it in the hayloft, only to have Frederick decide it was close to dry when he put a damp load of alfalfa and timothy into the barn hayloft only to have it heat up and ignite while they were milking the cows one evening in July 1932. Volkmar was the first to discover the smoke coming out of the horse barn hay loft and he ran back to the cow barn to alert Pop and Mom.

"Pop, there's smoke coming out of the horse barn! Should I let the horses out?"

"Ja! Und dann renn zum Auto Geschäft und ruft die Firewehr an und sag wehr haben einen fire Anfang im Pferde Schone!"

("Yes. And then go in the gas station and call the fire department that we have a fire in our horse barn!")

Volkmar ran as fast as he could and the gas station owner called the Chittenango Fire Department which came immediately. They turned their hoses on the house first of all since the buildings were just across the street and the house and immediately began to steam from the cold water upon the roof and sides of the house. They then turned the hoses on the horse barn and then the cow barn since the wind was blowing in an easterly direction. Volkmar had let the horses out of the horse barn and drove them down the road way towards the lower fields. He then headed for the cow barn in which Pop and Mom were already letting the cows and calves out and driving them down into the nearby fields away from the fires which were now breaking out in the cow barn and the silo. Pop was disappointed with the activities of the Chittenango firemen since they were directing their hoses on the water and milk shed and the house across the road. Pop could not understand why the firemen were directing so much effort on these further removed buildings while the fire was consuming the barns and silo!

"Why aren't you directing your hoses on the horse barn and cow barn?" He yelled as loudly as he could!

"Because those two buildings are already in flames and I don't think it's going to do any good to waste the water on them anymore! I've called the Fayetteville and Minoa fire departments to come and help us. We don't want your house to catch fire, too!"

Needless to say, not only the horse barn, cow barn and silo were consumed by the flames, but there was nothing left of the equipment which had also been inside the tool shed next to the horse barn. By the time the other two fire departments arrived, it was too late to do more than keep water pouring on the house across the street to make sure it would not catch on fire!

Pop was at a loss to know what to do next. He had a barn across the road, but it was not prepared for the number of cows he had nor where he might put his horses. As he was considering what he was going to do next, his neighbor from across the road some distance away found him and suggested, "Fred, why don't you put your cows in my barn? I've sold all of my cows and the barn and silo are filled with food that the cows would enjoy eating."

"Thanks Mr. Nesbitt. That would be a big help for me right now. There's nothing left to house them here anymore!"

And with these words, the Nesbitts and neighbors, who had been watching the fires, rounded up the cattle and drove them along the highway up to the Nesbitt farm along with the three horses. It wasn't very far, less than half a mile towards Chittenango. The cows felt right at home eating the ensilage and hay from the Nesbitt's barn and silo. Pop and Mom finished milking the cows and returned to the house in time for Mom to make supper for the family. Pop took two of the horses back to the house where he put his milk cans in the cold water of the cooling tank near where the fire had burned off the rest of the buildings. A neighbor had brought the milk cans to the Nesbitt barn where Pop poured the milk as they completed milking the cows. He then put the three horses in the shed behind the hay barn next to the house in which they became the barnyard next to the house.

Each morning, Pop and Mom rode up to the Nesbitt barn in the wagon drawn by Dick and Tom to milk the cows, and feed and water them before taking the milk back to the milk house where the delivery truck stopped each morning to pick up the milk cans to take them to the Chittenango Milk Factory. After a week of this arrangement, Pop asked Mr. Nesbitt what he was going to charge him for the use of his barn and feeding his cows and horses.

"It won't be too much, Fred. I think maybe two to three dollars a day should pretty much cover your costs for the use of my barn and the feeding of your animals."

Pop thanked him for the information and said he was going to have his animals auctioned off as soon as he could because he could no longer afford the cost of boarding them in the Nesbitt barn. Since Pop had bought an old Willys-Knight, he drove it over to his brother's house that evening and talked with him about contacting an auctioneer to schedule an early date to sell the cows.

"I certainly can't afford to keep the cows much longer in the Nesbitt barn, Karl. It's already cost me more than thirty dollars already and if this goes on much longer, I won't have any money left!"

"I'll go with you, Fritz, to talk with the man whose an auctioneer in Jamesville. He's the same man you bought your cows, machinery and equipment from when you first started farming."

"Okay Karl. That would be a big help. We'll visit him this next Saturday when you're done with your job at the Easy Washer."

On that next Saturday morning, Karl arrived at eight o'clock to drive Pop up to the auctioneer's house to discuss setting up a date for the sale of his eighteen cows so that he could pay Mr. Nesbitt for the use of his barn, hay, ensilage and water for his cows after the fire. The auction was held that next Saturday at nine o'clock in the barn yard of the Nesbitt farm. There were many farmers in attendance even though the advertisement was mostly by word of mouth. The neighbors had alerted the community about the auction and while it was only for the sale of fifteen cows and a couple of calves, the response from the community was impressive. Pop got an average of sixty dollars per cow (Holsteins) so that he could pay Mr. Nesbitt for the cost of his hay and ensilage but charged nothing for the use of his barn. Pop offered to pay him rent but Mr. Nesbitt said, "Don't worry about it, Fred. I've got more than enough manure to make up for the rental cost for the use of the barn!" he said as he laughed at his own joke!

The Next Earliest Days on the Farm

When we arrived on the farm in January 1929, the farm buildings consisted of the house, built in 1793, the horse barn, on the eastern part of the yard, the well, to the southeast slightly behind our garage, and the garden, to the south and west of the house, set off in a large yard with pear trees, plum trees, grapes and lilac bushes to the front of the garden near the highway. There was also a large thorn bush just outside of the living room window towards the western end of the house. There were also chestnut trees just in front of the house. A rain catcher covered the porch on the front of the house. There was also one of the largest elm trees we had ever seen growing on the eastern end of the house between the sidewalk and the driveway spreading its limbs towards the south, the west (over the ends of the house), and over the highway to the north. There were no longer any branches extending from the elm tree towards the east due to the fact that the limbs had broken off years before and the opening had been covered by concrete spread over the space where the eastern limbs had broken off. The stump of the tree was more than thirty feet in diameter. It was by far the largest tree we had ever seen except for a few still remaining in our northern woodlot.

The horse barn was for the horses that pulled the stagecoaches along the highway in the previous century and they were kept overnight in the basement of the barn separated from the basement floor by a three inch think ceiling keeping the hay for the horses above them. The water for the horses was kept in the twenty-two foot deep well just to the eastern end of the garage. While the water was hauled to the water tank daily from the water pumped from the well, it eventually was fenced off just to the south of the pump where the water was then pumped directly into tubs placed inside the barnyard fence which kept the cows and horses in the extended barnyard and pasture beyond the pump where the water was then pumped directly into the tubs placed inside the barnyard fence which kept the cows and horses in the extended barnyard and pasture on the nearby fields and hills.

The barns across the highway (on the north side of the highway) were huge by local standards. There was a huge horse barn, workshop, and storage area just across the street from the western end of the house. This is where the horses were housed over the winters. There were two blind horses (Dick and Lady), black and white on their faces and a gray horse (Tom) which could see and each time my father wanted to catch him in the yard, he would run away and could only be caught when he ended up in the area between the rail fences which circumnavigated the entire farm and the fields in between. My father eventually decided to tie him to a wagon wheel with a rope and which the horse (Tom) then pulled around from pasture to pasture and water stream to drink as he wished. At least he could be caught when he was needed to work on the farm. The other two horses (Dick and Lady) wandered from field to field as well as they could since neither of them could see from their blindness. They were able to find the ponds and streams of water with which to quench their thirst as best they could. While Tom was by far the strongest horse on the farm, trying to catch him had simply become too onerous and, therefore, Pop simply tied him to a wagon wheel which he dragged around while eating whatever grass he could find to his satisfaction.

The horse barn was ideal for the horses. Tom had his own stall to which he was tied daily during the winter and only taken out to pull the manure wagon each morning to one of the fields where Pop spread the manure. He only used Dick and Lady when he wanted to make sure they would be most useful and helpful when he took his oldest son along with him to spread the manure. Tom had a tendency to want to keep moving rather than wait until the manure from the cow barn had been spread by pitch fork.

The horse barn was divided into three separate sections. On the western end, the horses were tethered to the walls from which they ate their hay and occasional grain. There was actually room for four horses along the rear wall but Pop only had three. Therefore, there was on space in which he kept his grain which he occasionally fed his horses. In the winter, he led the horses out to the well on the eastern end of the barn yard to let them drink from the tank which he pumped full each time he had either his horses or his cows out in the barn yard. He had to tie Tom to the well shed so that he wouldn't try to run away and he had to lead him back to the horse barn and tie him into his stall each time Tom had had enough to drink. Dick and Lady weren't a problem. They simply stood and waited until Pop led them to the water tank which he had pumped full for them to drink.

Just behind the area in which the horses were tethered, was a work shop in which Pop could work to repair his equipment or tinker with his machinery to run more smoothly. Just beyond his workshop there was an outdoor wagon cover under which Pop could store his hay in the event of a rain storm or simply to store his wagons to keep them dry when not in use.

The really big barn was the cow barn in which he had fifteen cows which he and Mom milked by hand each morning and evening. The barn was built facing east and west so that the cows were in the barn yard to the south of the barn when they went out side of the barn to drink water from the tank next to the well on the north side of the road next to the highway. I still remember sitting on a stool between the two rows of cows being milked by my parents while watching them as they moved from cow to cow. On one occasion Mom was so sleepy she sat down next to the bull at the end of the row of cows on the right hand side and Pop walked up to her and laughed "You're not going to get much milk out of him!"

On the eastern end of the barn sat the biggest silo in Onondaga County, we were told by the salesman who sold the farm to Pop. It towered over the barns and the base of the silo is still recognizable even today (September, 2017) from the concrete which was poured shortly after the beginning of the 20th century. The silo filling took

GROWING UP ON A FARM

place with the help of our neighbors when they also had the help of Pop. It was the custom of these days that each farmer helped his neighbors and they then helped them in doing the same. Since Pop didn't have a corn harvester, he depended upon his neighbors to cut the corn into the bundles which were then picked up by the horses and wagons as the farmers pitched the bundled corn on the wagons to take it to the silo filler at the silo and was then thrown into the filler which chopped up the corn which was then blown up into the silo for winter storage and distribution each day during the winter season. My older brother, Volkmar, had the job of throwing down the ensilage to the base of the silo in the cow barn where Pop then distributed the chopped up corn to the cows as they stood in their stanchions and waited for the chopped up corn. I used to sit on one of the milk stools on the platform where the ensilage was thrown down while Pop and Mom milked the cows. As they moved down the line of cows to milk, I would move my stool along the center of the barn between the two sides of the gutters to watch as they milked the cows. In contrast to the cow barns which we later built, the center corridor was made of wood as were the gutters and the areas where the cows stood and slept. The aisles leading into and out of the cow barns were also all made of wood.

As we look over the remnants of the barns since the era of the 18th century in which these old barns were built, concrete has replaced the wood not only where the cows stood and slept, but in the aisles leading into and out of the cow barns. One additional feature which I found later to be rather unique about this old wooden cow barn was the huge door leading out to the north of the barn and looking down into a low spot in the field just below the cow barn. This opening had a large door which was open occasionally on hot days and which was used to throw out the manure from the gutters until a large pile of manure had accumulated which was then loaded into manure wagons and taken out to the fields to be distributed for fertilizer. I remember one day when my parents had completed milking the cows, Pop was driving them out of the barn when one of the cows turned towards this open door and jumped out of the door into the manure pile some feet beneath where she landed. It took her some time to gradually retrieve her feet so that she could walk off the pile unto solid ground again. Pop never left the door open after that until the cows had all left the barn through the regular entrance into the barn yard!

I should also mention it was just on December 10, 1928, that I was born in Syracuse, New York in the Catholic Women's Hospital on Grand Boulevard. My father had already decided he had had enough of the different attempts to find jobs that were of interest to him and in which he was understood by the employers. The purchase of a farm was totally new to him. He had never even visited a farm in Germany in all of his years of living there. He literally had no idea how to work a farm or even how to milk a cow! Fortunately for him, he had a neighbor (whom I've introduced earlier), Frank May, who lived just two farms to the west of us on Route Five, who also had a problem with his speaking capabilities and took an interest in this new neighbor. Frank May literally became his teacher, neighbor and friend who taught him how to care for his cows and horses and what crops to plant and how to prepare each field for the various types of crops he was to raise for his animals! One of the hardest but most important jobs which Frank taught Frederick was how to milk his newly purchased cows!

As I've mentioned earlier, were it not that Frank May had observed Richard Hausmann driving the wagon with the horses, tools, and equipment on the wagon from Manlius and had then followed him to the farm to introduce himself, Pop's introduction to farming could have been a disaster! Frank was very helpful in not only putting the cows into the stanchions, but also in helping Pop and Richard to learn how to milk the cows that first night in the barn! It was the start of a training program which was of enormous help to Frederick and Richard for their initial introduction to farming which they only recognized years later had begun with this initial introduction of their neighbor by his helpfulness. Fortunately for Pop and Mom, my arrival had helped the Hausmanns to decide to come to the farm to help in doing the necessary work which could only be done by them since Mom was so busy taking care of me as the newly born Megnin baby!

It also meant that Uncle Richard and Aunt Margaret had decided to move to the larger of the two houses on the farm in order to establish a tourist home for travelers using the New York Route Five state highway as their major means of travel eastward to Albany, New York City and New England or Rochester, Buffalo or westward to other western cities. It was the start of an adventure which none of them had had any idea would occur. It also meant that Grete, the younger daughter of the Hausmanns, would walk each morning to the Mycenae School House with Volkmar and Inge to attend school. The Hausmann's son, Richard, had entered the College of Forestry in Syracuse and, subsequently, remained in their house in Syracuse, New York.

That first summer was an exceptional introduction to farming for Frederick Megnin and Richard Hausmann. Since neither of them had ever farmed nor were familiar with farming, had it not been for Frank May, their experiences in learning how to farm could had been disastrous! Frank seemed to check on them almost daily to make sure they were doing the right things with the cows, horses, and crops in the fields.

The farm consisted of three large farm buildings on the opposite sides of the road from the farm house. On the extreme west was the horse barn, a large building capable of housing four horses with their own hay barn just over head and ample room for wagons to keep them under the roof on the eastern end of the barn. Since Pop had only three horses, he had room to store his grain and tools in the empty space reserved for the fourth horse. The horse barn was just across the road from the western end of the house. The cow barn was the next barn just to the east of the horse barn. Here Pop had stanchioned his fifteen cows and calves facing north and south inside the barn with the gutters flowing east and west in their wooden troughs with the largest silo in the county abutting the eastern end of the barn. As a little boy, it was my privilege to sit on a stool just where the silage was thrown down from the silo during the milking period and then periodically I would move my stool along the central runway as my parents moved from cow to cow to milk them. I was too young to attend the milking sessions of Pop and Uncle Richard but did so of Mom and Pop after the Hausmanns returned to their home at 207 Knaul Street in Syracuse, New York.

One of the first tragedies that was experienced on the farm was the fire which started in the horse barn hay mow. It was late in the afternoon of July 1932, that Volkmar came running into the cow barn as Mom and Pop were milking the cows.

"Pop!" Volkmar yelled out as he came into the cow barn. "The horse barn is on fire! Should I let the horses put?"

"Ja, sicher! Und dann geh hinunter zum Benzine stelle und frag der Gesschaeftman er sol die Firewehr anrufen and sagen einen von unseren Schonen ist im flammen!"

"Yes, indeed! And then go down to the gas station and have them call the Chittenango Fire Department and tell them one of our barns is on fire!")

Volkmar did as he was told and then came into the cow barn again to help Pop drive out the cows before the cow barn caught fire. Volkmar drove the cows and horses out into the nearby pasture. Then the Chittenango Fire Department finally arrived as did the Kirkville and Minoa Fire Departments to try to control the fire from spreading across the street to the house. The house was saturated with water so that it literally steamed. The Minoa Fire Department kept spraying the house and also the shed on the north side of Route 5 since it was so close to the burning barn and silo. The constant showering of the well shed kept it from bursting into flames as the other buildings had done from one barn to the next. It did mean Pop was able to keep the water tank as a useful addition across the road in the rear of the building which he built over the well. The upshot of the total burning of all of the buildings on the north side of the highway was that Nesbitt told Pop, "Fred, you can put your cows in my barn since its empty. There's plenty of hay and ensilage in my barn and silo so you shouldn't have any problems feeding your cows as much as they need. Subsequently, Pop and the neighbors drove the cows up to the

Nesbitt farm and installed them in an abundant location with plenty of food and water for the cows. It was only close to a month later when Pop asked Mr. Nesbitt, "What are you going to charge me for boarding my cows and calves with you, Mr. Nesbitt? They are eating heavily from your hay and ensilage."

"Oh I guess maybe two or three dollars a day should be plenty. So don't worry about it, Fred. There's plenty of time before Spring comes around and the cows will be back out on pasture."

Pop thanked Mr. Nesbitt and then decided at that rate of repayment, he would soon run out of money. He arranged with his brother, Karl, to visit the auctioneer in Manlius from whom he had purchased the cows to arrange a time for an auction to sell his cows and young stock as soon as possible. It was that next week that the auction took place and Frederick sold all but three of his cows and calves ranging from sixty dollars per cow to ten to fifteen dollars per calf at the auction. He kept his favorite Holstein heifer and all black Holstein cow, and another spotted Holstein in order to rebuild his dairy after he had rebuilt another cow barn adjacent to the hay barn which he still had on the same side of the street as the house. It was then that he took Tom and Dick down into the Schlucht (valley) each day to cut down the Hemlock trees which he then had the horses pull up to the field just behind where the cow barn had stood. It was here that he decided would be the best place for a sawmill to be set up to cut the trees into boards, two-by-fours, two by sixes, two by eights and two by twelves for the building of a new cow barn next to the hay barn which stood next to the house on the south side of Route Five. It was that next year that Pop hired the sawmill owner to come to the farm and saw up his collection of logs which he had gathered behind where the cow barn had originally stood. He had also hired Carly Leach, who lived in Mycenae, to work with him not only to saw up the logs which Pop had cut, but also to help him rebuild a cow barn so that he could once again have a monthly milk check to deposit in the Chittenango State Bank.

Overall, Frederick was pleased with the progress he was making in rebuilding his barn and anticipating once again to have a supply of milk to send to the Queensborough Milk Company. Fortunately for Frederick, he had made enough from the sale of his cows at the auction to be able to hire Carly and begin rebuilding his new cow barn. They worked together in digging out the base of his new cow barn walls to a depth of three feet and a height of five feet for the wall on the eastern and southern sides of the new barn. The northern wall was just four feet high including the first part which was three feet in the ground.

It should also be mentioned, the fire, which started in the horse barn, simple continued to ignite not only the cow barn, but then also the silo. When Pop asked why the firemen were not hosing the cow barn after the fire broke out in the horse barn, their answer was "We really can't contain the fire on the north side of the road. The only thing we can do is try to prevent it from spreading across the road and setting fire to your house! It looks like what we are doing is going to work. Your house is only steaming, it's not burning anywhere, Mr. Megnin!"

And with that explanation, the firemen from Chittenango and Kirkville kept their hoses trained on wetting down the house from the front to the rear. It never caught fire.

It should be noted that by September 1929, the Hausmanns were already through with their interest in sharing the work on the farm with Pop and Mom. The Hausmanns had decided the tourist business without indoor toilets and bathrooms was not for them. They told Pop and Mom that they were going back to the city and said the big old house was theirs to use and they could rent out the small house in which they had been living. Needless to say, Pop and Mom were greatly disappointed but, since they had no other option, accepted the Hausmanns departure with some degree of anger and disappointment!

It should also be noted that Grete, the Hausmanns teenager who had been attending the local school in Mycenae with Volkmar and Inge was now withdrawn from that school and enrolled in a grade school near Knaul Street where the Hausmanns lived. Volkmar and Inge had to walk back and forth from the Mycenae school to the farm alone since Pop had no car in which to take them back and forth. Previously Volkmar and Inge were accompanied by Grete and now they were once again alone!

Since this was the time of the Great Depression of the 1930s, not only had Frederick and Emily received very little money for the milk they were producing, but generally all farm products were selling at a very minimum price! There were men on the street everyday seeking something to eat from Mom and asking if they might have something to do to pay back the cost of the food which they were consuming. Invariably Mom turned them down and simply gave them a sandwich and an apple or a piece of pie, if she had made one. They were very thankful and Mom told us not to stand around them while they were eating because they would usually ask for another sandwich or piece of cake if one of us was standing around watching them eat their lunch. Another of the privileges which the men often asked for was

"Can I spend the night in your hayloft until morning and then I'll be on my way?" Pop usually allowed them the privilege to do so with the caution, "There's no smoking allowed in the hay barn!"

"Oh don't worry about that! I don't even have any money to buy cigarettes!" And usually Pop allowed them to climb up to the hay mow to spend the night sleeping in the hayloft.

Unfortunately, Frank May warned Frederick about making sure the hay was dry before putting it into the hayloft, only to have Frederick decide it was close to dry when he put a damp load of alfalfa and timothy into the horse barn hayloft only to have it heat up and ignite while they were milking the cows one evening in July 1932. Volkmar was the first to discover the smoke coming out of the horse barn hay loft and he ran back to the cow barn to alert Pop and Mom.

"Pop, there's smoke coming out of the horse barn! Should I let the horses out?"

"Ja! Und dann renn zum Auto Geschaft und ruf die Firewehr Geschaft und sag wehr haben einen Fire Anfang im Pferde Schoane!"

("Yes. And then go down to the gas station and call the fire department that we have a fire in our horse barn!")

DONALD F. MEGNIN

Volkmar ran as fast as he could and the gas station owner called the Chittenango Fire Department which came immediately. They turned their hoses on the house first of all since the buildings were just across the street and the house immediately began to steam from the cold water reaching the roof and sides of the house. They then turned the hoses on the horse barn and then the cow barn since the wind was blowing in an easterly direction. Volkmar had let the horses out of the horse barn and drove them down the farm road towards the lower fields. He then headed for the cow barn in which Pop and Mom were already letting the cows and calves out and driving them down into the nearby fields away from the fires which were now breaking out in the cow barn and the silo. Pop was disappointed with the activities of the Chittenango firemen since they were directing their hoses on the water and milk shed and the house across the road. Pop could not understand why the firemen were directing so much of their efforts on these further removed buildings while the fire was consuming the barns and silo!

"Why aren't you directing our hoses on the horse barn and cow barn?" He yelled as loudly as he could!

"Because those two building are already in flames and I don't think it's going to do any good to waste the water on them anymore!"

After the Sale of the Cows

Pop kept three cows from the eighteen that he originally had. Two Holsteins, a mostly black one and a mostly white one, plus the young Holstein heifer which impressed him with her growth and sharp demeanor in protecting herself when she drank at the water tanks. Even some of the older cows didn't bother to contest her for access to the water tanks when they also wanted to drink. They simply waited until she was through and had left the water tanks when she had had enough.

One of the first jobs that Pop undertook, besides cutting down hemlock and spruce trees in our woods and hauling them up behind where the cow barn had been, was to make room for the cows under the hayloft in the basement near the house. He dug a long gutter across the back of the barn on the first floor which he then blocked off with wood and poured concrete in it to make the gutter permanent and erected three stanchions in which the cows would be kept while being milked or over the winter months. He also made sure there was enough room for him to place hay and grain in front of the cows with stanchions to make sure they would remain there for longer periods of time as it might become necessary. He placed the horses in the covered shanty which he had attached to the rear of the hay barn and made an area out of which they could eat the hay which he placed in front of them and the occasional oats or grain he gave them as his money permitted. It was from this lean to shed behind the barn which had been used to tether the horses pulling the stagecoaches in the nineteenth and early twentieth centuries along Route Five, which became the shed in which the horses were kept each year when not on pasture. He took Dick and Tom down to the woods and began to cut down hemlock, spruce, ash and maple trees into twelve foot length logs which he had the two horse pull up into the field just behind where the cow barn had stood. After amassing more than two hundred of these logs, he hired a sawmill owner to bring his sawmill over to his field of logs and set it up to saw the logs into two by twelves, two by sixes, two by fours and inch boards with which to construct a new barn for his next herd of cows. As I've mentioned earlier, he had hired Carly Leach, from Mycenae, to come and work on the farm with him and especially to help him build his new barn on the east side of the hay barn to the southeast of the farm house where we lived.

Since Pop had closed down the gas station and pumps had been removed, the rock cutter along Chittenango Creek up towards the Chittenango Falls, stopped and talked to Pop about renting the gas station shed and the nearby lot in order to sell his beautiful rocks which he had dug out of the creek and creek side hills below the falls. Pop thought this was an excellent idea and agreed to rent his building and local grounds for him to set up his displays. He did an excellent job displaying his deeply etched rocks not only in the office space, but in the nearby yard. Mom had planted a ring of flowers near where the cars had stopped to have their gas tanks filled from the nearby pumps. The stone cutter than proceeded to set his ring of etched rocks just outside of the ring of flowers which set them off beautifully for everyone to enjoy. (The stone cutter's sons managed the business and included housing a small ice cream and candy shop in the building from which they could oversee the rocks displayed outside on the porch and along the roadway and adjacent lot which had been our camping ground for persons who wished to park overnight on their long trips to Albany, New York City and New England.

On one occasion a group of gypsies pulled into the camping ground and asked if they might spend the night. Pop agreed and they set up their tents behind the rock sales displays and used our outdoor toilet facilities at the end of our garage behind our house. The gypsies liked the area so much they asked if they could stay longer than overnight. They were willing to pay the nightly fee and after a few days some of the ladies asked Mom if they could use her sewing machine to mend some of their clothes. She allowed them to do so with the proviso that they do their sewing on the porch behind the house. This system worked for a few days when they asked if Mom had any extra thread and patches they could use to mend their torn clothing. Mom had also noticed that the gypsy children were going into our garden behind the house and helping themselves to the fruits and vegetables which were growing so well in our garden. Needless to say, Mom was upset by this taking off with her fruits and vegetables from her garden and told Pop about it. He said he would talk to the Gypsy leader, which he did. It was also in this time frame that the sons of the stone cutter complained that some of the Gypsy children were taking candy off of their counters and not paying for them. Pop talked to the Gypsy leader and warned "If you don't keep your children out of our garden and if they don't pay for the candy that they take from the boys in the stone shop, then you're going to have to leave."

"I'll talk to the parents," the Chief said. "We like your place here and we'd like to stay longer."

The Chief talked to the parents about the thievery from the garden and the rock shop, but it continued. The Stone Cutter told Pop he was losing too much money to theft to make it worth his while to continue to rent the display space from him.

"If their thievery doesn't stop, I'll have to call it quits, Fred!"

Pop went over to the Chief and said, "I've had enough complaints from my wife and the stone cutter about what your boys are doing to her garden and their business. I want you to leave this afternoon or I'm calling the State Police and have you evicted. I can't have all of this stealing going on for which nothing is paid!"

"Okay, Fred, I'll tell my friends we'll have to leave. We've enjoyed being here very much. You've got a really nice place for campers, but if you want us to leave, then we'll have to go!"

The Chief then went to each of the tents and told the guests to pack up their things and take down their tents. "Fred doesn't want us here any longer!"

Within an hour the Gypsies had taken down their tents, packed up their cars, and had driven off towards Chittenango and eastward.

The Yearly Megnin Event

One of the earliest occasions that I can remember of having all of our relatives on the farm was over the fourth of July, 1935. It was the annual meeting for the 4th of July picnic which the Frederick Megnin family hosted each year for relatives and friends to celebrate the annual holiday which pleased everyone who attended. The relatives and friends included the Karl Megnins (Karl, Anne and Billie), the Hausmanns (Richard, Gretel, plus Dick, Billie and Susan Weiss), Klumpps (Karl, Sophie and Hilde), the Dietzes (Karl, Sophie and Richard), Mr. Nicke (Tante Elise and Wally), plus our family: Pop, Mom, Volkmar, Inge, Fritzle (Donald). There were tables and chairs set up in the camping ground under the large elm tree plus the beer barrel and wine bottles so that no one was left with nothing to drink should their glasses become empty!

The Purchase of Goats

In the mid-thirties, Pop decided to buy some goats. He thought if he sold goats' milk, he would have a more expensive product and receive more per quart than from cow's milk. He wrote letters to the various hospitals in Syracuse only to have them write back, they would be glad to receive such a supply of goats' milk, but he would have to deliver it daily to the hospital. Since Pop had neither a truck nor a car large enough to convey such products, there was no way he could deliver the goats' milk even if the hospitals where willing to purchase. Needless to say, he wasn't going to buy a truck for this occasion (he could not afford one), so he simply let his calves drink the goats milk from the goats themselves. He built a milk stand upon which the goats were kept in a stanchion while the calves sucked the milk from the goats. It worked well for the caves, but the goats suffered through the repeated head butts of the calves trying to draw more milk from the goats after they had finished their attempts to retrieve more milk after they had drained the goats!

After Pop and Carly Leach had completed building the first new cow barn adjacent to the hay barn on the east side of the house, Pop decided it might be a better idea to milk the cows on the north side of Route 5 rather then to have to drive the cows across the road twice a day and take chances on whether or not the large trucks could stop in time as the cows were crossing the highway. He did have a few instances where some very large trucks had been unable to stop in time and had run into a couple of cows that were ambling across the highway each evening. Invariably the cows had to be sold to one of the butchers who drove by each day and stopped to find out if Pop had a cow or a bull calf to sell from his herd. If the cow had died shortly before the butcher stopped to inquire if he had any cows or calves to sell, the butcher would buy the cow and put her into his truck to take he to the slaughter house to complete the slaughter and drain the insides while hanging up the rest of the carcass to cut into various sizes he wished to sell to the nearby butcher and meat shops.

As I've already indicated, when Pop bought the goats, he thought they would be an asset to the local hospitals in Syracuse for patients having a need for a higher caliber of milk as part of their diet. He then notified the hospitals indicating he had goats milk available for patients. They immediately wrote back and indicated they would be pleased to have him ship a daily supply, however, they were not in a position to have the milk picked up and shipped to their hospitals. He would have to make these arrangements himself. Since he had neither a car large enough to do so, not a truck to make such deliveries, he was left with his only option as I've mentioned: giving the milk to calves, cats and dogs!

An Incentive to Buy a Sawmill

Pop decided since Volkmar had studied forestry, he should buy a sawmill so that they could harvest the many trees in both the woods above the hill and down below where he had cut down so many trees that became part of the cow barn which he and Carly Leach had built. Pop had bought a 1936 John Deere model B tractor which he used to provide the power to run the sawmill only to discover it was not powerful enough to do so. He decided to buy a heavier tractor, a John Deere model BR from the John Deere dealer in Manlius to run his sawmill. Once the neighbors heard Pop had bought a sawmill, one of them, Harold Fox, from Mycenae, drove over to the farm on his tractor pulling three big logs he wished to have sawed into wooden blocks to use in building a bridge over the creek which ran through their farm.

Volk and Pop set up the sawmill and hooked up the BR tractor to the sawmill and after rolling one of the logs on the saw mill, they put the log in line with the saw. The saw started to cut into the elm log but after going about five inches into the log, the tractor stalled. They started the tractor up again and after brining the log back out of the saw, proceeded to try again with the saws going through the section already sawed. As soon as the saw hit the section which was still not sawed the same thing happened: the tractor stalled and both Volk and Pop decided they didn't have enough power to complete sawing the log into any usable sizes. They started up the tractor again and moved the log backwards and dropped it off to the side of the sawmill. Volk walked over to the Fox farm and told Harold what had happened.

"I'm sorry Harold, but our tractor just isn't strong enough to saw up your logs into the sizes that you wanted. We'll have to get a bigger tractor one of these days and try it again!"

Harold drove his tractor over to our farm, hooked his chain around the ends of the three logs, and dragged them home again. It wasn't until four years later that Pop and I bought another John Deere tractor (Model A) which was able to provide the power necessary to run the sawmill.

Volkmar Leaves for College

In the Spring of 1937, Volkmar completed his high school education attending Fayetteville High School and with a very promising high school record wanted to go to college. The Syracuse University College of Forestry appealed to him since his older cousin, Dick Hausmann, had graduated from there in 1932. Pop told Volkmar he didn't have enough money to send him to college but suggested he talk to his sister, Gretel Hausmann about helping him to go to the College of Forestry. Volkmar talked with both his aunt and uncle and, since they had helped their son go to college, they knew what costs were involved.

"Volkmar, wir können Dir helfen. Du kannst bei uns wohnen und mit der Strassenbahn nach der Universitate fahren."

("Volkmar, we can help you. You can live with us and use the streetcar to go to the University.")

"I'll pay you back, Tante (Aunt). I'll enroll in the ROTC program and when I've completed my education in the College of Forestry I'll go into the Army and pay you back for what you spent on my education.

The reason Pop suggested he should talk to his sister was due to the fact that both she and her husband had full time jobs. Since they had helped their son to graduate from the College of Forestry they knew what it would cost. Volkmar lived with the Hausmanns for the first two years and in his third year, he met another College of Forestry student, Dave Caldwell, from Canastota, who offered to pick him up sat at the farm each day as he drove to the College of Forestry in Syracuse. This worked out well for both Volkmar and the family. It

GROWING UP ON A FARM

meant he was at home and could occasionally help on the farm when he had time after completing his daily studies. His aunt and uncle continued to pay his bills at the College of Forestry so that Volkmar had no difficulty keeping up with his studies and occasionally helping out with the farm work when he had time to do so. In 1939 Pop got a job working for a German factory owner in Syracuse who not only could talk with him in German, but understood him when he explained what had to be done in German to manufacture the parts for American tanks at the beginning of World War II. Pop did so well working for this German factory owner that when he was offered a higher paying job as a tool maker he began working for the Continental Can Company making spare parts for American tanks throughout World War II.

Volkmar graduated from the College of Forestry in May of 1941, but since he was not yet twenty-one years old, he could not be inducted into the U. S. Army as a Second Lieutenant. He was not yet old enough to become an officer in the U. S. Army in those days. His Colonel told him, "Lieutenant, go on back home and when you're twenty-one, we'll be in touch with you to enter as a Second Lieutenant in the Army. We've got your name and address and we know where you live on the farm so we'll be in touch with you after you're twenty-one years old."

Subsequently, Volkmar became a full time farmer for the next year and one half undertaking the operation and full time work on the farm from early morning until dusk each day until the first of August, 1942 when he received his letter from the ROTC Colonel to enter the U. S. Army as a Second Lieutenant.

It was in this time period that Volkmar became the boss of the farming operation in 1941-42. He and Mom milked all of the cows twice a day. Pop rarely had to help since by the time he returned by bus from Syracuse each evening, it was almost six o'clock. By then Volk and Mom had milked all of the cows and Mom had made supper at which time we all sat down to eat. It was on one of these late afternoons that we had a visit from an old neighbor who worked on the Green farm (which was later purchased by Mr. and Mrs. Ned

DONALD F. MEGNIN

Mann Senior in 1942) adjacent to Green Lake State Park. Mr. Green and his wife had been drinking and after he came into the house (his wife stayed in the truck), he sat down next to my sister, Inge, who was visiting from her job in Syracuse. While she was drinking coffee, Mr. Green had been drinking rather heavily and as he sat next to Inge reached over to her knee and let his hand move up her thigh. Inge was rather disturbed by his behavior and after Mom asked him to move to a different chair and when he failed to do so she said to me, "Donald, geh hinaush and hull Volkmar. Der man tute nicht was ich Ihm sag!" (Donald, go out to the barn and get our brother. This man doesn't do anything I say!)

I left the dining room and went out to get Volk and told him what Mr. Green was doing to Inge. He came into the house and immediately told him, "Mr. Green, you'll have to leave right now! We don't allow such behavior in this house!"

"What do you mean? I'm only sitting here next to this young woman?"

"That's exactly why I'm asking you to leave! Either you'll have to leave or I'm going to have to throw you out! Do you understand what I'm saying? You don't put your hand on my sister's leg!"

"Listen here, young man! I'm going to tell your father what you did and he's going to get angry with you!"

"I'll tell you once more. Either you're going to leave, or I'm going to throw you out of the house!"

"Okay, okay. I'm on my way. I'm going to tell your father what you did to me the next time I see him!"

"Go ahead and tell him. He would have done the same thing if he were here!"

And with these parting words, Mr. Green took his leave before Volk would have thrown him out! Mr. Green got into his truck with his wife and drove off. He never returned for a second visit!

Volkmar became the boss of the farm. After the corn, which he planted, came up he decided it needed to be cultivated to protect the corn from the weeds. Volk harnessed Dick and put me on top of him.

GROWING UP ON A FARM

"You're going to drive him up one row after the other until we've completed cultivating the whole field. I'll help you get on Dick and then you'll steer him up each row while I guide the cultivator until we're finished.

He helped me mount Dick and then we proceeded from one row to the next. If I didn't keep Dick exactly in the center of the row, he yelled

"Get him in the center of the row and keep his there!"

I tried my best but this was newer good enough for my brother!

"Keep him in the middle of the row, damn it! If I have to tell you once more I'm going to give you a swift hit on your butt!"

Needless to say, I had several hits before we were through cultivating his new crop of corn! I told Pop about it that same evening after he came home from work. And all he said was, "Du muss halt besser aufpassen, Fritzle. Der Goal ist Blind und er weist nicht wo er geht. Du musst ihm im Mitte halten!" (You have to be careful. Fritzle. The horse is blind and he doesn't know where he's going. You have to keep him in the middle of the row.)

And so it was. I explained what I was trying to do in English and my parents replied to me in German. To Volk's credit, he did the best he could under the circumstances. It was only the help that couldn't match what he required!

61

Trying to Find a Good Use for a New BR Tractor

It should be noted that when Pop and Volkmar bought a new BR tractor in the spring of 1941 to plow the front lot along the highway from our farm to the edge of the Kelly farm line on the western side of our front lot on the north side of Route 5, the road, and lot down to the ditch, which had been used for years to drain the front fields had been located behind our barns on the north side of the highway. This tractor was also to be used to run the sawmill which they had decided to buy. This field was well drained on the eastern half of the field while the western half had an underground creek which flowed diagonally down to the ditches which led into the lower Kelly fields. Volkmar not only plowed and harrowed this field, but spread winter wheat seed over it which, in the following spring, produced an excellent crop of wheat to be combined in the summer of 1942. Ted Fox was the major combine operator in the area at the time and after I talked with him to come and combine our winter wheat, he came. But after he looked over the whole field said, "I'm not going to combine the western half of this field! It's too wet! I don't want to get stuck in there! I'd never get out without a big tractor pulling me through the mud!"

By the time Ted came to combine the wheat, Volkmar had all ready been called into the Army and Ted wasn't going to have me try to get someone to pull him out of the mud should be become stuck in the remaining part of the field which he refused to combine. In retrospect, it was an abundant amount of wheat which we used to feed our cows through the winter months. But over the next seventy five years, this western half of the front lot has never been plowed or used again to plant crops! Only the eastern half has been used for crops or for hay over the years since then!

Along the back lot bordering the woods to the north, a batch of new trees were beginning to grow into the edge of the field. Using a new tractor (the John Deer BR) which Pop had bought to run the sawmill in the spring of 1941, Volk thought he would use the new tractor and plow this part of the lot in the early spring through these new seedlings which had begun to grow on the northern edge of the field abutting the woods. These young trees bent over when Volkmar drove over the larger saplings. Not only did the tractor lean over in making headway plowing through the small trees which had begun to grow on the edge of the field, but these trees turned over rather well. When he hit the larger saplings, not only did the tractor lean to the left or right as he drove over them, but usually one of the rear wheels was off the ground having been tipped by the strength of the young saplings so that the tractor was left hanging on one side while the other rear wheel was still on the ground slipping on the edge of the saplings and going no where! He then dismounted from the tractor after putting it into neutral, took out his sharp knife from his pocket and cut the new sapling at the stump just at ground level and dragged it into the woods. He then had to raise the plow to get over the newly cut stumps and threw the cut saplings into the woodlot. He did this repeatedly and eventually cut all of the new saplings off, While it was not possible to plow through these underground root systems, it at least prevented the new trees from extending the wood lot further out into the field. As a consequence of cutting off these new young trees, he kept the field clean for the next years to plow through these root systems which had died after he had cut them off. To the eastern part of this back lot he had gotten approval from Pop and the College of Forestry to plant spruce and pine trees along the edge of the woodlot which covered the creek and the adjacent field which was too steep for a tractor to drive along safely. About one thousand of these young saplings were planted along the edge of the woods overlooking the creek bed at the base of the woodlot. Unfortunately, many of these

DONALD F. MEGNIN

trees never grew to adulthood since the hunters who came through the fields in the fall and winter cut them down for use in their homes at Christmas time. Less than a dozen of these saplings ever grew to adulthood. After Volkmar entered the Army in the summer of 1942 and Pop continued working at the Continental Can, there was no one who could impress the outsiders that such a subtraction of ever greens was not tolerated! The saplings were simple too far from the house and hidden behind the woods for anyone to notice what was happening to them. By the time Volkmar returned to the arm in late 1945, the damage to the number of trees had already begun. Each year fewer and fewer of the Christmas trees survived!

Another of the episodes which took place when Volkmar was actively engaged in farming after completing his College of Forestry Degree, was the cutting down of cedar trees in the woodlot with which to replace fence rails which had been broken or rotted through the years. This was one of the activities which we undertook in the winter once the ground was covered with snow. The tractor wasn't much help since the snow clung to the steel wheels and made it impossible to drive through the snow. Subsequently, we walked down to the back woodlot with a crosscut saw and axes to cut down the trees and haul them out of the woods by hand. It was a slow and hard job which we recognized had to be done before spring in order to have the limbs available to replace those that had rotted or broken over the years. The entire farm had rail fences from the highway to the wood lots. It was our good fortune to have relatively few broken rails along our fences. Needless to say, however, each year there were a few rails which had to be replaced mostly to keep our bull from crossing over into our neighbors' pasture to try to breed his heifers! Invariably, Volkmar and I would find rails which had been broken from the bull attempting to jump over them to attempt to breed Jack Benson's heifers! Mr. Benson wasn't very pleased with such activity on the part of our bulls since Holsteins produce more milk than do Guernseys! Having his Holstein heifers bred by our Guernsey bulls was not very beneficial to the expansion of the milk production by his holstein heifers when they became cows! Hence, we had to repeatedly check on the status of our bulls as we let them out to pasture with our cows near where Mr. Benson pastured his heifers! Needless to say, Volkmar and I did cut down several cedar trees, chop and split them into rails, and replace the broken rails as they were needed. We soon discovered Mr. Benson had decided to replace the wooden rail fences, where were broken, with barb wire and fence posts rather then rail fences!

An Unusual Birth

It was late in the afternoon one summer day in 1941 and the cow that was supposed to have given birth to a calf that day still hadn't come down from the hill pasture next to the woodlot. Volkmar suggested, "We'd better look for the cow. She should have come down to the barn by now with her calf."

We walked up the roadway to the top of the hill and into the fields just before the woodlot. We walked along the field next to Murray's pasture up to our woods behind the hilltop lots. We walked along the woods and as we approached the end of the second field, we saw the cow grazing along the front of the woods.

"Well, there she it," Volkmar said. "But where's the calf?"

As we approached the cow we could see one foot of the calf sticking out of the cow's uterus.

"Where's the other foot?" Volkmar asked. "We better drive her drown to the barn and see what's the matter with the calf! There should be two feet sticking out. Evidently one foot is caught inside the cow."

We drove the cow down to the cow barn and placed her in an empty stanchion. Volkmar proceeded to push the other leg of the calf into its mother's uterus so that he could reach in and pull both feet out simultaneously. He then reached into the cow's uterus and got hold of both feet and pulled them out of the cow with the dead calf at his feet. Unfortunately, the cow's uterus also came out as well as from which Volkmar separated the calf and pushed the uterus back into the cow. The problem soon became apparent. Each time the cow had to urinate, her uterus came out as well. When Pop came home from

66

work that evening, Volkmar showed him the cow and the same thing happened each time the cow urinated.

"We better call the veterinary and have him come and take a look at her. She's a really good cow giving lots of milk. He can tell us what we should do with the cow."

Pop went back into the house and told mom to call the veterinarian in Chittenango to come and take a look at our cow. She went over to Kelly's and called the veterinary who said he would come up that evening. After he arrived, he and Pop went out to the barn to check on the cow. Her calf's litter box was hanging in the gutter as she was lying down.

"Well, I'll have to sew a couple of strings across her vagina, Fred. If her bag keeps hanging out it will become dirty and infected so that she will never be able to have any calves again. Actually, she'll never have any more calves since the part of her vagina, which is hanging out, indicates it has been torn away from the inner part of her uterus."

"You mean she'll never be able to have any more calves again?" Pop asked.

"That's what I'm saying, Fred. She'll be a good milk producer this year, but she won't be able to carry any more calves. There's no way she can become pregnant again since her uterus has been disconnected from the inner part of her uterine system."

"You mean I'll have to sell her for beef?"

"That's exactly what I'm saying. She can't produce anymore calves.

The veterinarian placed two strings across her vagina so that the uterus would no longer fall out. Pop sold the cow to the butcher that fall since she couldn't produce any calves any longer.

Putting the BR tractor to Good Use

It should be noted, however, that Volkmar did use the model BR tractor to plow the front lot along the highway from our farm road to the edge of the Kelly farm line on the western side of our front field and down to the ditch which had been used for years to drain the front fields which had been located behind our barns on the north side of the highway. This field was well drained on the eastern half of the field while the western half had an underground creek which flowed diagonally down to the ditches which led into the lower Kelly fields. He not only plowed and harrowed it, but spread winter wheat seeds over it which the following spring produced an excellent crop of wheat to be combined in the summer of 1942. Ted Fox was the major combine operator in the area at the time and after I talked with him to come to combine our winter wheat, he came but after he looked over the whole field said, "I'm not going to combine the western half of the field. It's too wet. I don't want to get stuck in there. I'll never get out without a big tractor to pull me through the mud!"

By the time Ted came to combine the wheat, Volk had already been called into the Army and Ted wasn't going to have me try to get someone to pull him out of the mud should he become stuck in the remaining part of the field which he refused to combine. In retrospect, it was an abundant amount of wheat which we used to feed for our cows through the winter months. But over the next seventy-five years this western half of the front lot has never been plowed or used again to plant crops! Only the eastern half has been used for crops or for hay over the years since then.

Creating Building Materials

It was in the early summer or 1936 that Pop hired Harold Coon and his crew to saw the logs which he had cut down in the woods and had hauled into the area just behind where the original cow barn had stood. It was here that the sawmill owner had set up his operation to saw the logs into two by fours, two by sixes, two by eights and one inch boards from the logs Pop had pulled into this area with his two prize work horses, Tom and Dick. He kept the sawmill operator busy by pulling up the logs as they were sawed according to the lengths Pop desired. After a three week operation, the logs were all sawed into the lengths Pop wanted and where he had stacked them to dry before starting the operation to build the new cow barn. Pop had borrowed money from the Chittenango Bank with which to once again build a dairy operation. He could buy cows and produce milk which he could once again sell to the Queens Borough Milk Operation in Canastota. The milk was shipped to the City of New York where the milk was distributed among the residents in various parts of the city.

With the help of Carly Leach, the building of the barn was concluded in time for the cows to be bought at a few auctions and kept in the newly built cow barn in the early days of September. We still had the original gas station stand from which Pop had originally sold gas and oil upon purchase of the farm in 1929. When the Hausmanns left to return to the city in September of 1929, he ended his contract with the gas company since he was no longer able to staff both his dairy operation and the gas station simultaneously. It was another year before Pop ended his contract with the stone cutter so that he could use the camping ground for his cows after they were milked.

Our New Neighbors

By the end of World War II, the Spencers had decided to sell their house and property and move back to a town or a village. They sold their home and property to the Parks family. Mr. Parks was a representative of an insurance company. He and his wife had two boys, Dickie and Billie. The names of the two parents were Richard and Jo Parks. Dickie was the older of the two boys and at age four enjoyed coming over to the farm and watching me as I milked the cows or cleaned out the barn. The Parks also had a big black, curley-haired dog who used to follow Dickie over as he came to watch me milk in the barn. Dickie liked to sit on the stairs leading to the second floor of the barn and and watch what was going on in the barn. I enjoyed Dickie's visits except for the fact that quite often his dog followed him and then a fight would ensue between Blackie and Adolf, our younger dog who was the product of a match which began between Buddy, Volkmar's dog, and a man who thought Buddy was a pure-bred German Shepard. Since Buddy looked like a pure bred, neighbors would have their females bred by Buddy thinking they would have a purebred German Shepard. What people did not know was the fact that Buddy had once followed Volkmar home after a Scout meeting in Kirkville and Buddy simply followed Volkmar home and never left. Adolf had been the product of a match between Buddy and a neighbor's dog whom the neighbor thought, since Buddy looked so much like a purebred, he wanted a series of pups who would also look like purebreds. What Volkmar didn't know, nor did anyone else, Buddy was evidently not a purebred, even if he looked like one, so when the owner of the dog whom he had brought to be bred by Buddy produced Adolf with his long ear flops, Volkmar decided to keep him.

On one occasion, as Dickie came into our yard around the corner of the house, Blackie bite me as well as fighting Adolf. I still have the tear line on my arm where Blackie had torn my skin with his teeth. I finally separated the two dogs after a couple more bites from Blackie before Dickie took Blackie home after I told him to leave his dog there. I retired to the house and had my bitten arm treated and patched because of the damages done to my left arm and hand. Mr. Parks had driven over to our yard and as Pop and I sat in his car and discussed what should be done under the circumstances, I was willing to let things gradually calm down without making much of a fuss about what I suffered.

"If Dickie wants t come over in the future, he should lave Blackie at home. I don't want to leave Buddy and Adolf in the house when we go out to the barn to do our chores."

"Okay, fair enough," Mrs. Parks said. Pop was outraged!

"What? You should go see a doctor and have your wounds treated? The Parks dog attacked you! You didn't attack the Park's dog!"

I got out of the car and thanked Mr. Parks for coming over.

"Don't worry about it, Mr. Parks. I have a couple of bites, but they'll heal. You better tell you wife that when Dickie wants to come over to the farm, he should leave his dog at home!"

"I will, Donald. Sorry what Blackie did to your arm. You'd better have a doctor look over your bites so that they don't become infected. I'll alert the doctor in Fayetteville to expect a visit from you."

Pop had already exited the car when I told Mr. Parks, "Don't worry about what happened. My arm will heal."

"If you want a doctor to look at your arm, Donald, I'll alert our Doctor in Fayetteville to expect you."

"No, that won't be necessary. It'll take a little time, but it'll heal," I told him.

A New Use for the BR Tractor

Along the back lot bordering the woods to the north, a batch of new trees were beginning to grow into the edge of the field. Using the new tractor which Pop had bought to run the sawmill in the spring of 1942, Volk thought he would use the new BR John Deere and the plow in this part of the lot in the early spring by applying the plow on the new seedlings which had begun to grow on the northern edge of the field, next to the woods. These young saplings bent over when Volkmar hit the larger saplings. Not only did the tractor lean over in making some headway plowing through the small trees which had begun to grow on the edge of the field, but these turned over rather well. but when he hit larger saplings, not only did the tractor lean to the left or right as he drove over them, but usually one of the rear wheels was off the ground having been tipped by the strength of the young saplings so that the tractor was left hanging on one side while the other rear wheel was still on the ground slipping and going nowhere. He then dismounted from the tractor after putting it into neutral, took out his sharp knife from his pocket and cut the new saplings at the stump just at ground level and dragged it into the woods. He then had to raise the plow to get over the newly cut stump and threw the cut sapling into the woodlot. He did this repeatedly and eventually cut all of the new saplings off. While it was not possible to plow through these under ground root systems, it at least prevented the new trees from extending the wood lot further out into the field. As a consequence of cutting off these new trees, he kept the field clean for the next years to plow through these root systems which had died after he had cut them off. The eastern part of this back lot

Pop had given approval as well as the College of Forestry to plant spruce and pine trees along the edge of the woodlot which covered the creek and the adjacent field which was too steep for a tractor to drive along safely. About one thousand of these young saplings were planted along the edge of the woods overlooking the creek bed at the base of the woodlot. Unfortunately, many of these tress never grew to adulthood since the hunters, who came intro the fields in the fall and winter, cut them down for use in their homes at Christmas time. Less that a dozen of these saplings ever grew to adulthood. After Volkmar entered the Army in the summer of 1942 and Pop continued working in the Continental Can, there was no one who could impress the outsiders that such a subtraction of evergreens was not tolerated! The saplings were simply too far from the house and hidden behind the woods for anyone to notice what was happening to them. By the time Volkmar came back to the farm in November of 1945, the damage to the number of trees had already begun. Each year fewer and fewer of the Christmas trees survived!

Another of the episodes which took place when Volkmar was actively engaged in farming after completing his College of Forestry degree was the cutting down of cedar trees in the wood lot with which to replace fence rails which had been broken or rotted through the years. This was one of the activities which we undertook in the winter once the ground was covered with snow. The tractor wasn't much help since the snow clung to the steel wheels and made it impossible to drive through the snow. Subsequently, we walked down to the back wood lot with a cross cut saw and axes to cut own the trees and haul them out of the woods by hand. It was a slow and hard job which we recognized had to be done before the spring in order to have the limbs available to replace those that had rotted or broken over the years. The entire farm had rail fences from the highway to the wood lots. It was our good fortune to have relatively few broken rails along our fences. Needless to say, however, each year there were a few rails which had to be replaced mostly to keep our bull from crossing over into our neighbor's pasture to try to breed his heifers! Invariably Volk and I would find rails which had been broken from the bull attempting to

DONALD F. MEGNIN

jump over them in his attempt to breed Jack Benson's heifers! Mr. Benson wasn't very pleased with such activity on the part of our bulls since Holsteins produce more milk than do Guernseys. Having his Holstein heifers bred by our Guernsey bulls was not very beneficial to the expansion of the milk production by his Holstein heifers when they became cows! Hence, we had to repeatedly check on the status of our bulls if we let them out to pasture with our cows near where Mr. Benson pastured his heifers! Needless to say, Volkmar and I did cut down several cedar trees, chopped and split them into rails, and replaced the broken rails as they were needed. We soon discovered that Mr. Benson decided to replace the wooden rail fences, which were his responsibility with barb wire and fence posts to keep our bulls out of his pastures!

Volkmar and Eva Return to the Farm

It was in November of 1945 that Volkmar and Eva retuned to central New York with their first born son, David, to once again take up the work on the farm which Volkmar had intended to do following World War II. One of the first tasks that Volkmar undertook was to buy the equipment to place a shower and a hot water tank in the kitchen to improve the conditions to make possible a hot shower and a flush toilet as an adjunct to the kitchen in the large front room to the west of the house along Route 5. Unfortunately, Volkmar and Pop also wanted to expand the cow barn in order to increase the number of cows they were milking. Hence, the newly acquired shower pipes and equipment was left in the hallway to the front of the house and was looked at each day as everyone entered and exited the hallway to go out to the pump and barn. They did succeed in adding on a barn addition from the western end of the hay barn to the eastern most end where the cows could enter the barn from the main part of the barn yard. They erected twelve stanchions along the back of the hay barn, shortened the silo, and gave an exit to the cows on the eastern end of the walkway so that the cows could enter and exit from the additional space for this second cow barn. Pop and Volkmar attended another auction and bought two large Ayrshire cows and two heifers to augment their dairy operation later in the spring. It gave them twelve cows by the end of April and eight heifers to augment their milk check considerably since these additional cows could be added to the milk check each month. Unfortunately, Volkmar never did get time to install his shower and additional pipelines into the house to improve the living conditions for his wife and growing family. They had their second son on June 8, 1946, which made it more difficult for Eva to care for her growing family without access to running water and the conveniences to which she was used to in her parents' home in Minnesota. By the time fall came rolling around (early September) she told Volkmar

"Pete, if you want to continue to work with your Dad and invest in this farm, then that's your decision! But as far as I'm concerned, I'm going back to Minnesota! I've had enough of this farm and with the equipment you men are using it's becoming more and more dangerous for David's safety! I'm going to leave on the 15th of September. I'm not going to stay here any longer! It's too dangerous and I don't want to have to take a bath after everyone has gone to bed! That's not the way I was brought up!"

"What" You want to leave the farm just as we're getting started in expending our operations? I'll get to installing the shower after we have the rest of the hay cut and put into the barn!"

"I'm sorry, but I can't wait any longer! Either you're coming with me, or I'm going alone with the boys!"

"I'm sorry but I can't stay wait any longer! Either you're coming with me, or I'm going alone with the boys!"

It was a long night for Volkmar in trying to persuade his wife not to leave the farm. The discussion lasted more than two days and finally Volkmar told Mom and Pop what he was going to have to do.

"I can't let Eva take the boys alone back to Minnesota, Pop! I'm going to have to look for another job! I'm sorry to do this to you, but maybe Fritz can help you out. He's finished high school now and he wasn't accepted at Syracuse University. Maybe he'll stay and help you on the farm."

And with this tearful discussion with Mom and Pop, Volkmar, Eva, David and Bob left in their jeep, a trailer loaded to the gills with boxes of toys, clothes and equipment Volkmar had purchased for us in the future, they made their three day trip to Minnesota to live with Eva's parents until Volkmar found a new job.

I should mention that while Volkmar and Eva lived with us in 1946, he often let me use his jeep to visit my friends at school over a weekend. There were lots of hills around DeWitt in those days and those of us who had jeeps took our friends out for rides in the nearby hills. Bull DuPree and I had the availability of jeeps most often. We took our friends, who didn't have such vehicles available to them, to the nearby hills and rode up and down them by the hour. Since we preferred the tops down it meant we could see better where we were going and how high the hills were that we were climbing. Another of the sports was Bill DuPree driving his Dad's Pontiac four door sedan going over 100 miles per hour down New York Route 20 from Cazenovia down another ten or twenty miles east before turing around and driving us back home to Fayetteville or DeWitt!

Driving the Cows Across the Road

We drove the cows across the road twice a day. Once in the morning after milking them in the barn each morning after they had spent the night on the hilltop grazing during spring, summer and fall. The rest of the time the cows spent the winter months in the barn and we only let them out after breakfast for an hour or so. On one occasion, we were driving the cows across the road at four thirty p. m. and were planning on milking them at five o'clock that afternoon. The cows moved quickly across the road except for a heifer which broke away from the herd and began running down the road towards the county line. I gave chase after her and finally got her turned around. She headed up towards the barn where the rest of the cows were waiting to gain entry into the cow barn. Pop opened the barn door and the cows wandered in and took their regular stanchions including the heifer that had run down the side of the road. Once she was locked into her stanchion, Pop picked up a board and began hammering her buttocks something fierce. I grabbed the board from him and he swung at me with his fist. I stopped him before he could hit me and took the board away from him, although he did break my glasses when he swung at me. I grabbed them before they fell to the floor and I told him, "Well, now you've done it! I'll have to get a new pair of glasses!"

With these last words, he turned and left the barn. Mom and I had to milk the cows ourselves that evening! I fully expected he wouldn't help that next morning, but he did. He even woke me up by banging on the stove pipes leading through my bedroom into the chimney!

Building a New Barn on the North side of Route Five

Since Pop had a large garage to the rear of the house next to the outdoor toilet, he thought he could use the lumber from this building with which to build a cow barn across the road from the rest of the buildings. He talked this project over with his brother, brother-in-law and neighbors with whom he had become acquainted following his arrival from Germany in 1927. They agreed it would be a good idea and promised to come to the farm on the next Saturday to dismantle the garage from the back of the house and rebuild it across the road where the original barn has been built years before. (It has burned down in 1932.) The dismantling of the garage only took one Saturday and was hauled by the horses and wagon across the road and piled next to the place where Pop had decided the next barn should be located. It was in the exact spot where the original barn had stood before the fire had destroyed it. The next Saturday the same crew of uncles, friends and relatives, Karl Megnin, Richard Hausmann, Karl Klumpp and Billy Weiss came out to the farm and helped Pop and Volkmar begin the project of building the barn in which to milk the cows twice a day. Pop had designed what was to be constructed so that each person knew how and where to begin and what had to be done to complete the project. Pop still had lumber left over from the original project of building the new barn on the south side of the highway next to the old hay barn so that he had plenty of lumber with which to complete his project.

It took the crew two Saturdays in which to complete the project since they had to construct the interior of the barn with stanchions,

DONALD F. MEGNIN

and areas in which to put the hay or grain should Pop decide to supply the cows with such incentives. The new barn proved to be useful for that next year when Pop got a job as a tool maker in Syracuse. When Tom Brady stopped by to ask if he might be interested in having him take over the operation of the farm on a monthly rate, Pop was intrigued. He thought it over for a day and decided that was the best thing he could do since Volkmar still had another year of college and Donald was still in grade school. The result was that Joe and Jimmy Hall, the two sons of the Hall family that lived next to the Bradys on the Green Lake road and worked for Tom Brady, simply took over the milking duties twice a day and plowed and planted the crops in the spring. Tom paid the monthly fee for the use of the Megnin farm from January to January 1939-1940. Pop no longer wanted to continue this arrange-meant during Volkmar's last year in college since he could help with the milking and care of the cows prior to going with Dave Caldwell each day to attend classes in the College of Forestry. Dave was a year behind Volkmar and since he commuted daily to the College of Forestry from Canastota, he offered to pick Volkmar up daily as he drove up Route Five to the University.

The New Adventure: Goats

As I've already mentioned, during the 1930s Pop bought a flock of goats which he thought could produce milk for those persons having problems with their digestive systems in the various Syracuse hospitals. While it was a very valid idea for persons having stomach ailments, without a truck to make daily deliveries, the hospital directors thought this was a requirement for the milk supplier and not that of the hospitals. Hence, as I've already indicated, he used the milk to feed his growing colony of calves instead of supplying the needs of human patients.

Pop had plenty of room when he converted the back room of the house to become a barn for his overflow of goats. He had been able to put four goats on the east side of the cow barn and the rest of them he placed in the back room next to where the garage had once stood. It was here that he also tied his growing calf problem since they were used to suck the goats dry twice a day. He simply carried over the bales of hay to feed the goats and carried buckets of water twice a day for the use of the goats. If he had more goats' milk than he needed for his calves, he simply put the rest of the goats' milk into the milk cans which he used for his cows' milk. He never had any complaints from the milk plant about the mixture of milk so that he continued to do so whenever he had an abundance of goats' milk.

What was so intriguing about the herd of goats was, who would take care of them? Volkmar was in college and too busy to spend any time with them. I was too young and my parents didn't want me to have to keep running after them once they were put out to pasture. Hence, that left only my sister, Inge, who could be designated the

DONALD F. MEGNIN

"Goat Watcher for the Megnin Family!" It meant that each Saturday and Sunday Inge had to take over the responsibility of letting the goats out to pasture, watching over them so that they did not go into our neighbor's garden and see to it to bring them home after spending the day out on the hillside or hilltop pasture. While school was in session, Inge had to attend classes and couldn't take the time off to make sure the goats would stay in our pastures. The problem with the goats was that they preferred to eat the apples or the crops being grown in our neighbor's garden to the west of our property. It was always a struggle for Inge that once she had taken the goats out to the hillside pasture and she had found herself a good seat on a stump or a rock, the goats seemed to wait until she was comfortably settled before they would race for the neighbor's fence and squeeze through the barb wire fence to feast on the apples or other delicacies of the neighbor's garden! It was then an effort for Inge to get off her comfortable seat, close the book she was reading, and race after the herd of goats who had made themselves comfortable in their neighbor's field or garden! When I was ten or eleven, she recruited me to go with her and she would send me after the errant goats feasting on our neighbor's crops! The problem was I had no one who could rally to my cause and suggest that was Inge's job! Either I had to go along and chase after the goats and bring them back home, or she got mad at me and threatened what she would do to me if I didn't help her bring the goats back home! On one occasion the goats were all in the field on top of the hill when it started to show blasts of lightening and the beginning of rain drops when she said "Donald, go round up the goats and drive them down to the barn before it rains even harder!"

By then the rain had really started to fall rather heavily. I chased them through the barb wire fence and as I was about to follow them I ducked low over a barb wire strand that stood a few inches above the ground and cut not only my shorts, but my scrotum on one of the barbs and tore a hole in my pants and scrotum which began bleeding rather profusely. I didn't stop until I was at the bottom of the hill and had helped her put the goats into the barn. It was then that she said, "What happened to you? You're bleeding right through your shorts!"

GROWING UP ON A FARM

"I must have gotten caught on one of the barbs as I ran through the fence."

"Well you better go in the house and tell Mom. Your shorts are all bloody!"

I ran into the house and told Mom what I must have done getting the goats together to drive them down to the barn during the rain storm.

"Sags Dye Vater. Er kann es vielleicht zubinden. Du hast schon viel Blut verloren, Donald!" (Tell your father. He should cover it up. You've already lost a lot of blood!)

I found Pop in the workshop and showed him my bloody pants.

"Wir müssen deine Hosen ausziehen und sehen was passiert ist!" (We'll have to take off your pants and see what has happened!)

He set me up on the living room table and pulled down my shorts to see what had occurred to make so much blood appear on my shorts.

"Du hast einen Loch in deinem Sack. Ich werde es abputzen so das wir sehen können wie Büß es ist!" (You have a hole in your scrotum. I'll clean it off and see what's happened to you.)

He proceeded to do so and then poured merchurekrom on the wound before he put a plaster over the wound.

"So, jetzt muss Du aufpassen das Du es nicht abreist von deinem Sack." (Now you'll have to be careful not to tear off your plaster from your scrotum.")

He lifted me gently off the table and helped me pull up my pants. It only took a few days to heal and Pop checked the wound each day to make sure the plaster over the scrotum wasn't torn off. After a week, it was no longer necessary to have it bandaged. Fortunately, the tear was only a small one. We could see the one ball in the sack and the wound was only a small one which Pop had plastered shut so that there was no danger of it falling out of the scrotum after it was taped shut.

My First Encounter with Wildlife

I was about ten years old when I walked down the field across from the house to see what Volkmar was doing further down the field. As I walked along the hayfield next to the roadway leading to the northern most fields of the farm, a young woodchuck came bounding across the field towards me. I stopped and noticed he wasn't stopping. I turned and ran towards the fence along the roadway. The young woodchuck kept coming towards me. Not knowing what he might do, I picked up a stone and threw it towards him. I didn't hit him so he kept coming towards me. I circled back to where the stone had landed and picked it up again. Since the young woodchuck kept coming towards me I picked up the stone again and this time I hit him on one of his paws. He quickly turned back to his hole in the ground and since he was only part way down I dropped the stone on his head. I didn't see him again after that. I've often wondered if I had not tried to keep him from me whether or not he could have become a friendly woodchuck and a wild animal friend had I but given him a chance to do so!

When I told Volkmar about my encounter with the young woodchuck he said, "It was probably just as well that you hit him on the head with the stone. He must have had some kind of ailment to become that friendly with a human being!"

Selling Firewood on the Farm

When Pop and Volkmar cut firewood for sale to the general public, Pop stayed with the cordwood next to the north side of the highway in case anyone came by to buy a cord of wood or more. Volkmar and I had gone down into the north side of the woodlot to pick up another load of wood to be cut into cordwood size. Volkmar suggested I might like to drive the tractor back up to the road where we would deposit the split logs and tree limbs next to the buzz saw. I enjoyed driving the model B John Deere tractor with its steel wheels and cleats which cut into the ground. As we were approaching the saw which sawed up the contents which we had on the wagon, I wanted to get as close to the saw as possible in order to drop the wagon load near enough to make it possible for Pop and Volk to pick up each piece and saw them into the one foot lengths which they did with most of the wood sawed by them from these loads which we brought up from the woods. In order to get near enough to the saw, I had to drive up the roadway in order to dump the load next to the saw. The only problem was that a prospective customer had driven into the roadway from the road side gate. I tried to drive past him as well as I could only to have the wheel shaft, which stuck out beyond the wheel, caught the customer's rear fender and riped the fender in half. As a consequence, Pop gave the man a cord of firewood as compensation for what I had done to his fender! Needless to say, I didn't drive the tractor near the roadway again until I was fourteen years old! It didn't matter if I drove the tractor out in the hay fields or in the woodlot, I only couldn't drive it up near the highway if there was a car parked in among the rows of cord wood piled in cord after cord over the area closest to the highway!

Mr. Van Giesen's Special Dispensation for Donald to Work on the Farm

When Volkmar was inducted into the Army in the summer of 1942, Pop wrote our high school principal a letter requesting that I, his younger son, Donald F. Megnin, be allowed to withdraw from high school each spring in order to prepare to do the necessary work, such as spreading the manure, plowing, disking and dragging the fields to be planted for the fall harvest. Mr. Van Giesen replied he would approve of this plan provided that I return in June of each year in order to take my final exams with the rest of my classmates. If I passed, I could then continue on with my class into the next school year in September. If I should fail, I would have to drop back to the class behind the one in which I had been located. I then became a full time worker on the farm each spring and was successful in doing the necessary farm work each spring and, fortunately, passed my finals each June to stay with my class. I spread the huge manure pile, plowed the fields, and dragged them so that Pop could plant the annual crops and have them ready to harvest later in the year. One of our biggest fields was that known as the "backlot". In other words, the field furtherest from the barn. The neighbors next door were the Kellys and the Farrells (which had once been Frank May's farm) to the west of our farm. Since I had already plowed and harrowed the front part of the "backlot" earlier and Pop had already planted the oats, he told me to plow the back part of the lot so that he could plant buckwheat on it. I did so and noticed that squirrels were having a great time climbing through the trees overlooking the valley and creek just to the east of the backlot. I decided to bring my twenty-two rifle with me after lunch and see if I could shoot some of the many squirrels that I had witnessed that morning. Needless to say, I fired several rounds at the squirrels as they jumped from limb to limb, but I don't think I hit any of them since as soon as I started shooting, they disappeared into their holes in the trees and stayed there until late in the afternoon. By then I had had enough of the attempt to shoot some of them and since I didn't think I hit any of them. I completed getting the plowed field groomed for Pop to plant the buckwheat that next Saturday morning. This was the same procedure I used repeatedly from field to field: spread manure over the field, plowed and harrowed it, then dragged it. Pop then planted the seeds (broadcasting them), and then I would cover the seeds by using the tractor and drag to cover the seeds. Generally, this method worked rather well since Pop spread the seeds in a uniform system of throwing the seeds out ahead of him in a rhythmic system which meant uniformly in the distribution of the seed with each throw of his right hand.

Building a Place to Swim

Billy Megnin was about thirteen years old and I was about ten when he suggested we go down to the shlucht (woods) and make ourselves a swimming pool in the creek which flowed through our woods. We took an axe, a shovel and our good intentions with us. There was one part of the creek that had a relatively deep pool in the center of the creek which Billy thought we should exploit to our advantage. He used the axe to cut down some of the trees growing along the creekside and told me to dig out the sand and mud from under the water and throw it on the far end of the creek beyond the deeper center. I did so and he then placed the pieces of wood which he had cut on top of the mud which I had placed at the further end of the creek. The blocked water at the northern end of the flowing creek began to slow down the flow of the creek water and whereas we had only about two feet of water originally, we now had more than three feet of water and the level was still rising depending upon how much mud, dirt and stone we placed on the logs at the head of the creek. This dam held the water nicely when we kept adding dirt and stones to the content of the dam. When the water had risen to a depth of four feet, we both could dive into the pool and get completely wet. The only problem that we had was when we jumped into the pool, the force of the water pushed the dirt and stones further down the creek so that after a half an hour we had to rebuild the front of the dam in order to maintain the depth that we wanted for the purpose of diving into the creek. At any rate, we enjoyed the experience and after a couple of hours in our boy made pool, we could let the water continue to wash away the residue of the dirt and stones which we had used to dam the creek in order to make it possible to dive into the deepened pool. When we went down to the creek later that week, we had to rebuild the dam and add rocks and dirt to the wood pile which we used to dam the creek in the first place. We also learned that the more we dove into the pool, the more the dam at the other end would give way from the stress the waves forced upon the dam. After a few days of trying out our boy made pond, we discovered that the more we built on our dam, the more we had to strengthen it by repeating our efforts over and over again. We did discover that the use of wood as a barrier to our pool was the best way to deepen our pond. We did discover, however, that even with several of these wooden barriers at the top of the pond, the water kept pushing through usually by washing away the dirt and gravel which we had used on the dam. We learned that our swimming pond would only last a few hours before it was ultimately washed away from the pressure of the creek moving ever forward against whatever barrier we tried to erect.

Tom, Pop's Best Horse

Tom was about the best horse we had ever had! He was gray, strong and didn't like to be used for work on the farm! Whenever Pop tried to go out into the pasture to try to put a rope around his neck, Tom would take off and run to the other end of the field. Only the fence prevented him from escaping permanently! Pop finally decided the only way he could have him available for work was to either keep him in the horse barn, or tie him to something that would keep him from running away. Pop decided to move him to the barn and place his harness on him would not do justice to his horse. Pop decided having him nearby and available whenever he was needed was better than chasing him around the field and trying to coral him in one corner of the field. Pop had a wagon wheel which he decided was strong enough to keep Tom, from running away each time he approached him. Pop placed a rope around Tom's neck and tied it to the wagon wheel which he could pull around but prevented him from running away each Time he wanted to use him for a job. Unfortunately, Pop didn't keep Tom in the pasture in which he kept the other horses but placed him in a grassier field. It was an obvious treat for Tom, however, there were rocks and small trees in the field that could snag the wagon wheel and prevent Tom from moving wherever he wanted to go. One morning, when Pop wanted to use Tom to haul loads of wood from the woodlot to the buzz saw, he sent Volkmar down to get Tom to bring him up to the barn in order to put on his harness on Dick and drive them down to the woodlot to haul up the split logs and limbs and saw then into useable sizes for the customers. As Volk walked down to get Tom, he noticed he was

GROWING UP ON A FARM

lying down and not moving. As he came closer to Tom he saw why he was not moving. It had rained the night before and the gnarled rope has simply tightened around Tom's neck so tightly he couldn't breath anymore. He had simply collapsed and died from the rope tightening around his neck. The wagon wheel had simply been caught between a little apple tree and a huge rock from which he could not budge. Volkmar returned to the barn and told Pop what he found.

"Tom's dead, Pop. He was caught between a small apple tree and that huge rock at the beginning of the field. He couldn't move the wheel and in his efforts to try to pull away from the tree and rock, he was coked to death. It must have happened during the night because when I found him he was cold and wet from the rain."

"Das ist aber schade! Er whar der beste Pferd das wir gehabt haben und jetzt ist er Tod! Jetzt können wir ihn nur zum Sumpf zeehan. Es wahr nur einenge Wochen sein bis nur seine Beine ueberrich sint!"

("That's really too bad! He was the best horse that we had and now he's dead! Well, the only thing we can do now is take him down to the swamp and dump him in. It'll only take a few weeks before there is nothing left of him except for his bones!")

Volkmar and Pop went into the pasture where Dick and Lady were grazing and brought them back to the barn where they put on their harnesses and walked them down to the field where Tom lay. They also took the dual horse block to which they attached the chains to Dick and Lady's harnesses and placed a chain around Tom's neck. Pop than drove the two horses down the lane to the swamp next to the creek just to the north of where Billy and I had built our swimming hole that previous summer. When they arrived at the swamp, it was just beyond the area of the woodlot in which the creek flowed through the end of the tree line and opened between the woodlots. Pop drove Dick and Lady to the edge of the creek just before the creek flowed through the woodlot to the north of the swamp. Once he had unhooked the chain from around Tom's neck he and Volkmar turned Tom over a few times until he fell into the swamp from the edge of the hill bordering the creek. He would stay there until the wild life had eaten enough of him to leave only his bones which eventually disintegrated from old age. It was not a pleasant place to visit for several months because of the stench of the decaying flesh which the foxes, coons, dogs and other wild animals had feasted upon before winter covered what remained of his carcass.

It was only two years later Pop opened the horse barn door and found Lady lying dead on the ground next to the hay holder from which she had been eating her hay. Dick was standing next to her and continued eating his hay unaware that his fellow horse mate had died. This time Pop brought out his John Deere tractor model B and hooked her up to the draw bar with a rope around her neck and pulled her down to the creekside again as he had done with Tom. Again, the stench was overwhelming before enough of Lady had been consumed by the wild animals to leave only the fragments of bones around to indicate that another horse had been committed to its final resting place in the swamp.

As a consequence of the death of Lady, Pop had to decide what he should do. Should he look for another horse to buy and use with Dick around the farm, or should he create machinery useful for one horse rather than two! He decided that the latter option was the best since it was the cheapest and, besides, he had a tractor which he could use in case he needed more power than that provided by one horse. He had an old chassis from a car which he no longer had and decided to reconstruct it to use as the basis of a wagon which he would create for Dick to pull. He built an excellent wagon to be drawn by Dick to use around the farm, to haul bags of grain, tools, or wood depending upon how much he needed of each item. It was a two wheel cart which he could use whenever he had a small load which did not require a larger space. The cart worked out very well except from my point of view. It had a real limitation to it. Since Pop made the cart using the basic frame of the car around which to build the useful remnants into a two wheel cart. From the two long sides of the frame, Pop cut off the two long sides of the car frame at roughly half the length of each side as had been originally part of the car frame. This left an exceptionally sharp end on each side of the horse which would cut into each of his sides depending upon which way the horse would be driven. Pop tried to soften this damage to Dick's sides by placing leather covers over Dick's sides to lessen the damage which might have been done to Dick's sides. Nevertheless the bumping back and forth seemed to be very uncomfortable for Dick so that this useful cart which Pop had made for his horse was only sparingly used.

And Only One Horse Was Left

With only Dick as the survivor of the three horses, Pop had originally bought after buying the farm in 1929, it was only in the spring of 1942 that Dick died. He had spent the winter in the barn which Pop and the relatives had built in 1937 in the eastern end of the cow barn where the original cow barn had stood and which Volkmar had closed off in order to provide some warmth for Dick in which to spend the winters. Volkmar was still waiting to be inducted into the U. S. Army in 1942 since he was too young to be inducted as an officer previously. Since Volkmar was doing all of the farm work while Pop worked as a tool maker making parts for American tanks in a Syracuse factory. Volkmar had decided to close off the eastern end of the barn in which Dick could spend the winter. He fed him and watered him daily and even distributed some straw around one section of the space he had available for Dick in the eastern end of the barn. It was a cold day in March when Volkmar came across the road to look after Dick. He found him stretched out and dead as he opened the barn door. Dick had grown a luxuriant coat of hair over the course of the winter. As Volkmar was looking him over he decided it would be a good idea to skin him and sell his hide to the slaughter house along with his body after he had skinned him. He proceeded to do exactly as I've outlined although it took him all day to skin him correctly, but he felt he had done an excellent job. When he asked Mom to call the Rendering Company to come to pick up Dick's skeleton, she went over to Kellys and asked to use their phone. Mrs. Kelly gladly let her use their phone. Mom called the Rendering Company and they said they would send a truck out late that same afternoon to pick up the carcass. When the truck arrived, Volkmar took the driver over to the barn and showed him the skeleton.

"What happened to the skin?" the driver asked.

"I skinned him and I'll sell you the hide if you'll take it," Volkmar replied. "What is it worth?"

"We usually give five dollars for the skin of an animal that's been skinned. Let me take a look at it?"

Volkmar showed him Dick's hide and the driver was impressed.

"Tell you what, I'll pay you five dollars for the skeleton and ten dollars for the hide. It's about the best I've ever seen!"

Volkmar was pleased with the transaction and when he told Pop about it that evening, Pop was also quite impressed with this arrangement and thought Volkmar had done an excellent job in making a profit from this exchange!

Picking Cherries with the Relatives

Each summer the Hausmanns came out to the farm with Billie Weiss and asked Mom if she and the kids wanted to go with them to Murrays in order to pick cherries. Invariably Mom always said yes, she'd like to go. We then went in Billie's (Grete's husband' car) to the Murray farm and made arrangements to pick cherries in the quart baskets Mrs. Murray provided for the occasion. Once they were full they were poured into the bags the Hausmanns or Mom had brought along and paid ten cents a quart emptying them before handing them back to Mrs. Murray so that someone else could use the same baskets. Neither the Hausmanns nor the Megnins ever took more than five quarts each. Not only was it a hot adventure, but the cherries had to be washed and canned for winter storage in each of our cellars. The Murray's had a big cherry orchard just behind the cow barn which was fenced off so that the cows were kept out of the cherry orchard. There were also apple trees in this same fenced off acre so that the customers could pick both cherries and apples if they wanted. The apples sold for fifty cents for a large basket which again was emptied into a customers bag and the basket returned to Mrs. Murray.

With Only A Cow Or Two

Since the Murray farm was just to the east of us in Madison County, it was during this period of time when Pop only had one or two cows in the barn next to the house. So, whenever one of the cows was in heat, he tied a rope around her neck and walked her over the hill to the Murray barn where George kept his bull in his cow barn. Whenever Pop arrived at the Murray farm he usually tied the cow to one of the barn yard posts before going over to the Murray home to talk with George about having his cow bred.

After knocking on the kitchen door, George came out and he and Pop exchanged greetings and shook hands.

"Well, what is it today, Fred? Did you bring up your cow to have her bred by my bull?"

"Yes. It looks like she's in heat, that's why I've brought her over."

"Well, let's go over to the barn and I'll let my bull out to service her."

And without any further adieu, they walked over to the cow barn and George let his bull out into the barnyard where Pop had tied the cow. The bull moved quickly over to Pop's cow and sniffed her behind and then proceeded to mount her. After one or two thrusts of his penis into the vagina of Pop's cow, George's bull slid off Pop's cow and sniffed her behind where he had inserted his twenty-five inch penis. Usually the bull mounted the cow one or more times just to make sure the conception would take place. Both the cow and the bull seemed satisfied that the copulation had been successful and the bull had no objection to being driven back into the barn and to his stanchion at the end of the line of George's cows. He had done what

DONALD F. MEGNIN

was expected of him. Pop gave George the dollar bill for the service charge and Pop led his cow back to his farm again. Nine months later the product was either a bull or a female calf. Fortunately for Pop, he had his holstein cow give birth to two excellent female calves that proved to be excellent milk cows for the new crop of cows Pop was trying to create as the basis of his new herd of dairy cows. Pop's best cow as a Holstein and George's bull was a Guernsey so that he had two new cows which produced a higher butterfat milk for which he received a higher monthly milk check because the milk was of a richer quality.

One of our Guernsey cow's produced an outstanding bull calf which we raised with the expectation that he would become an excellent addition to improve our stock of milk cows. Volk was working on the farm at that time and he and Pop decided this young bull would be an excellent improvement to the stock of Guernsey cows if he were used for breeding purposes. They both wanted to let him out on pasture with the cows so that he could breed them as they became ready to produce new calves year by year. They let him out with the cows only to find that this young bull was attracted to the young heifers which Jack Benson was raising next door in a pasture abutting one of our own pastures. Since Mr. Benson had warned Pop that he wasn't going to allow his Holstein heifers to be bred by a Guernsey bull. He told him he had to make sure that our bill didn't try to jump over our wooden rail fence. In discussing what they should do, it was decided that Volkmar should plant a ring in the bull's nose in order to hitch him to a lead line and attach him to a tree or a pole to prevent him from trying to jump over our fence and attempt to breed the Benson heifers. Volkmar and Pop drove the young bull into the cow barn across the road from the barn which Pop and Carly had built and locked him into one of the stanchions which were used to milk the cows each morning and evening. Volkmar was busy attempting to thrust the screw driver through the nose of the bull when Roy May stopped by since he heard we were having trouble keeping our bull out of Jack Benson's heifer pasture. Volkmar was attempting to thrust the screw driver through the nose of the bull and having to continually tie the bull more tightly to the stanchion in which he had placed him. Needless to say, thrusting the screw driver into one side of his nose to push it through to the other side was difficult and hurt the bull enormously with each thrust that Volkmar gave to the screw driver.

Roy watched for a short time and finally said, "Let me try it, Volkmar. Maybe I can put it through better since I've done this a number of times with my own bulls. You've never down this before, have you?"

"No. This is the first time I've ever tried to do this." And with these comments he gave Roy the screw driver.

Roy placed his arm under the bulls' jaw and lifted it as high as he could before thrusting the screw driver through the bull's nose from one side through to the other.

"Well, that takes care of it, Volkmar. Do you have a ring to put into the bull's nose?"

"Yes. Here it is," and gave it to Roy. Roy shoved it through the one side of the hole he had made in the bull's nose and clicked it together.

"Do you have the two screws that hold the ring together?" Roy asked.

"Yes. Here they are." And with that Roy inserted the two screws into the nose ring and set the ring back into the center of the bull's nose so that the screws were hidden inside the nose.

"Where are you going to tie him up, Volkmar?" Roy asked.

"We thought we'd tie him to one of the telephone poles out here in the lot next to the barn."

"Not a bad idea. Be sure it's long enough so that he can run a bit when the cows come to visit him."

"I've got a fifty foot long rope now. We'll see it it's long enough."

Volkmar tied the rope to the telephone pole nearest the cow barn where it seemed to serve the purpose until one day when the cows started running before a severe storm hit. It was then that the bull began to run with the cows and instead of slowing down as he came to the end of his rope, he simply kept going only to have the ring rip out of his nose! We only noticed what had taken place after the rain stopped and the bull was no longer at the end of his rope, but among the cows waiting to go into the barn to be milked. The bleeding gradually stopped and it was simply impossible to catch him because each time Volk or Pop wanted to get near him he took off. They did finally capture him by having him come into the cow barn. He came into the barn to help himself to the grain which they provided for him along with the cows. This was only two days later and by then the bleeding from his nose had stopped. They tied a rope around his neck and head so that when he tried to run with the cows, he was simply pulled back by the rope on his head so that he could no longer run freely as he had earlier! He was then retied from one telephone pole to the next depending upon how much grass had been eaten by the bull. It was also interesting to note that some of the cows stayed near him while the others drifted off to parts of the field where the grass was much higher. Pop finally sold this bull when it was difficult to move him from place to place without two men holding on to the ropes attached to his head. It was simply one of those tragedies that could not be transformed except by using more men than it was worth to move him from place to place. It became simply too dangerous to move him about with only two men!

Getting My Arm Broken

After Volkmar entered the Army on August 1, 1942, it became my job to sit on Ted Fox's combine that summer to harvest the oats which had been planed earlier in the spring. In early September, I returned to Fayetteville High School to complete my freshman year. Waiting for the school bus after school was out of the day, a group of us who rode the bus went out to the playground behind the school. I was on the side of Bob Ford, Dale Holtz and Johnny Daniels while Francis Ford, Wayne Rasmussen, Tommy Brady and Freddy Holtz were on the opposing team. As our team huddled, Dale said, "Fritz, you go out to center field and I'll throw you a pass behind Wayne so that you can run across the end zone and score a touchdown!"

"Okay. It shouldn't be too hard to catch."

And with that final word in our huddle, I lined up across from Francis Ford and was ready to run out into the back of the opposing team's lineup. As the football was centered to Dale to toss the pass out to me, I started to run out and as I passed Francis, he stuck out his foot over which I tripped and landed on my left arm. I got up and my arm simply hung down my side. I couldn't move it. I told my teammates,

"I can't move my left arm!" It simply hung down my left side. Dale came over and grabbed it and pulled on it. It only hurt and I couldn't move it in any direction.

Dale spoke up and said, "Fritz, you better go in and see Miss Wagger. There's something wrong with your left arm. You can't seem to move it!"

Bob Ford went with me to Miss Wagger's office. She looked at my arm and tried to raise it which only hurt as she tried to lift it.

DONALD F. MEGNIN

"Well, tell you what, Donald. I'll drive you home and we'll see what your parents think we should do. You'll have to see a doctor and find out why you can't raise your arm."

And with that she said, "Let me take you out to my car and I'll drive you home. We'll have to hear what your parents have to say what we should do.

And with these final words to Bob, Dale, and a few of the others in the group with whom we were playing, Miss Wagger drove off for the farm.

As we drove into the driveway on the farm, we noticed Pop and Mom were just unloading hay into the hay barn. Mom was in the hayloft spreading out the hay as it was pulled into the hay mow. Pop had to push the hay fork into a part of the hay on the wagon, then climb down and mount the tractor to drive it forward so that the hay would be dragged up into the hay mow. He would then stop the tractor, climb up on the hay wagon and trip the rope so that the hay could fall into the mow where Mom would have to mow it away wherever there was a place to push it. Miss Wagger drove into the yard and parked the car near the back door of the house. She got out of the car and Pop had just backed the tractor back to the wagon to place the hay fork in another bundle of hay on the wagon.

Miss Wagger got out of the car and introduced herself to Pop. "Mr. Megnin, I'm Susan Wagger and I'm the Fayetteville high school nurse. I've brought your son home because I think he has a broken arm. He was playing football and another boy tripped him as he ran past him. He fell in some hard soil and I think he has a broken arm."

By then Mom had come down from the hay mow and introduced herself.

"Hello," she said to Miss Wagger. "I'm Donald's mother. Is there something wrong with him?"

"Yes. I think he has a broken arm, Mrs. Megnin. I think he needs to see a doctor."

By then Pop had come down from the hay wagon and came over to the car. He looked at me as I sat still in the front seat of Miss Wagger's car.

"What were you doing?" Pop asked.

"I was playing football and one of the boys tripped me as I was running past him! I can't use my arm. It hurts too much!"

"What in the world were you doing playing football? You know we don't have a car! The only way we can see the doctor is by bus!"

"That's all right, Mr. Megnin! I'll take him into the city and have a doctor at one of the hospitals take a look at him."

"Oh that would be a big help for us, Miss Wagger," Mom said. "Let me change my clothes and wash up a bit and I'll go with you to see the doctor."

"Take your time, Mrs. Megnin. I'll wait here with Donald until you're ready to go."

By this time, Pop had stormed off to finish putting the hay into the hay barn by himself. He didn't say anything to Miss Wagger as she drove off with Mom in the back seat and Miss Wagger and I sitting in the from seat. There was relatively little discussion of any kind as Miss Wagger drove into the city to the Crouse-Irving hospital. Mom was grateful that Miss Wagger had agreed got take us there, It would have been a long wait until we had a bus come by on Route 5 to take us to the city and several blocks we would have had to walk to reach the hospital from where the bus would have let us off.

Miss Wagger knew the doctors very well at the Crosue-Irving hospital. She took us to see Dr. Potter who was a specialist in treating broken limbs. He had the arm x-rayed and found out that the bone comprising the elbow had broken off from the rest of the arm.

"It looks like Donald has a broken elbow, Jane. I'll patch it up and after a three week period, it should be okay again."

And with this diagnosis, Dr. Potter proceeded to place my elbow into a caste and placed it into a bent position so that it could grow back together again. Upon completion of this operation, he said, "Well, Donald that should take care of it. You won't be able to play anymore football this season, but there shouldn't be any problem for you to play it next year!"

Dr. Potter told Mom, "Mrs. Megnin, I'd like to see Donald again in three weeks. He shouldn't get his arm wet. H should keep it dry and after three weeks, it should be mending as if he hadn't even broken it. Do you have any questions about what I've done?"

"No, I don't have any questions, Dr. Potter. I'm just glad you were here and that Miss Wagger was able to bring us to you so that Donald's arm could be fixed."

"You were fortunate to have Jane available, Mrs. Megnin. It's not every nurse that would have driven out to your fan with your son, brought you to the hospital, and is taking you both back home again!"

"Yes, we are fortunate in having Miss Wagger available to take Donald out to the farm and then here to your office and now back home again! It's not every nurse that would have done so much for us!"

After saying our good byes to the doctor, Miss Wagger took Mom and me back home again. Mom had been able to make a down payment for the doctor's services with the understanding that for the next visit she would bring the rest of the money in payment for the services which the doctor rendered. Mom also asked Miss Wagger what she should pay her for the time and effort she took to drive me out to the farm, pick her up, drive us to the doctor's office, and then back home again! Needless to say, Mom was overwelhmed with gratitude for the willing service, Miss Wagger had performed in our behalf. Pop, on the other hand, was angry no end that I had caused him this amount of agony and cost while simply waiting for the school bus to bring me home again!

Mom and I took the Syracuse-Utica bus line back and forth a few times to visit the doctor and have him check on the healing progress I was making under his direction. By the time, Dr. Potter was satisfied that my elbow had healed, Mom had also been able to pay the bills for my broken arm.

We had completed the building of the new cow barn and had the cows in the barn for the winter. We thought we had all of the problems solved by the middle of November so that the cows began to stay in the barn during the day and only went outside briefly for some fresh air and exercise. We noticed, however, that when a cow wanted to drink from her installed water holder nothing was coming out as she pushed her mouth down on the trip lever that produced the water in the water holder.

Pop suggested, "Donald, Du kannst vielleicht unser Leiter im Brunnen hinunter stellen und sehen weshalb wir koenen Wasser bekommen." ("Donald you can put the ladder down into the well and see why we're not getting any water!")

I got the ladder and opened the door over the well and placed the ladder down into the well. I climbed down the ladder and as I stepped off of it, I sank into several inches of mud. There was a little water here and there but nothing from which any water could be taken up the pipe to let the cows drink.

"Pop, why don't you hand me down a bucket and a shovel and I'll dig up the mud from the base of the well to make more room for water to flow in again."

Pop did as I asked and handed the pail and shovel down on the rope which I then took off the rope and filled the bucket with mud. Once I had filled it, I reeled it up to Pop to pull the pail of mud up to dump. He did so and then dropped the bucket down again. We did this for the next half hour and the water was slowly seeping back into the well. After an hour of digging out the mud and leaving a solid base for the water to accumulate, Pop said, "Feilleich waer es besser wenn wir einen Wassermann bestellen werden so dass wir genug Wasser haben für unsure Kiehe." ("Maybe it would be better if we contact a water driller and have him drill a new well for our cows.")

I climbed up the ladder and went into the house and told Mom what Pop had said.

"Mom, could you call the well driller over in Bridgeport and ask him to come over and drill us a new well so that we can hook up the new well for the cows to have water to drink?"

"Ja, das kann ich tun. "Yes, I can do that."

She called him and he said he would come over that next Monday morning after he finished drilling another well for a farmer in Chittenango Station. In the meantime, Pop and I drove the Jeep down to the creek in the woods and filled our old milk cans dull of water which we had filled from pail after pail of water from the same deep part of the creek where Billy and I had swum years before. After filling the eight cans of water, we drove back up to the barn yard, let the cows out, and Pop and I kept dumping the cans of water into the bathtub tanks which Pop had collected from earlier years when Uncle Richard and Uncle Karl had worked for the Easy Washer Machine Company. The tubs were castoffs from the factory deemed no longer salable because of checks and cracks in the sides or the tanks. Uncle Karl had simply brought them out to the farm because he thought they might come in handy for just such purposes as this.

The cows drank heavily from the creek water and we were fortunate in that we did not have to return to the creek to refill the cans again until the next morning. These watering tanks had stood outside next to the well with a long rail attached to the pump on the top of the well which was used to pump water into them from which the cows drank before we had installed the self-serving system in the cow barn next to each cow. Needless to say, the well did fill up again after a few days after we had had the new wells drilled next to the rear of the house. It still has an excellent supply of water which is not longer used except to carry pails of water for the flowers around the outside of the house.

Needless to say, I had to dig a new ditch in which to put the new pipe from the new well to the cow barn so that the cows could help themselves whenever they were thirsty. It was also at this time that we installed the piped water from the new well into the house for use in the kitchen, bath room and availability in the more distant parts of the house. Pop did all of the work and I simply assisted him whenever he needed help. The new well was only down forty-eight feet into the ground so that we were very fortunate to have relatively little expense in supplying the necessary water for the cows, the milk house, and the family house. Had Volkmar and Pop put in this water system earlier no doubt Eva would have been satisfied to stay on the farm longer than she did. But having to run out to the pump and get a fresh pail of water each time she needed fresh water in which to bathe one of her boys or cook some food requiring water had simply become too onerous for her to accept! Had the equipment all been purchased after Volkmar and Eva moved into the house in November of 1945, I doubt Eva would have wanted to move off the farm so quickly! However, this new equipment had simply been left on the floor to the entranceway in the rear of the house, which resulted in Eva demanding to leave the farm after September 15, 1946!

The Dangers of Cows Crossing Highways

After Volkmar entered the Air Force on August 1, 1942, it left only Mom, Pop and me to take the cows across the road to the barn each evening for milking purposes. Since Pop's eyes were not the best and he did not want to wear glasses if he were to enter the barn to milk the cows, he was in charge of letting down the bars on the roadside gate for me to herd the cows across the busy highway. Looking towards the west along the Route Five highway, most of the cars had gone past our gate and as Pop looked towards the west, there was only a huge tractor trailer truck moving down the roadway towards where we were driving the cows across the road into the barn yard before driving the cows into our barn to milk. The cows were slowly moving across the highway and this huge tractor-trailer truck seemed to have trouble stopping. In fact. he didn't really stop until he ran into one of our best milk cows and knocked her down on the street. We got her up again and we drove her across the road only to have her lie down again just before entry into the barnyard gate. after considerable effort, she got up again and we drove her into the barn to milk. In the meantime, Pop talked with the truck driver and he gave his name, address and phone of his trucking firm. The driver explained he simply couldn't stop any sooner since he had such a heavy load on board. He apologized and said Pop should contact his company and if the cow was hurt in any way they would reimburse him for the damages. After another lie down of the cow in the barn yard, we got her up again and we drove her into the cow barn. After a few minutes she laid down again and while we milked the other cows, she died. The butcher, who usually stopped almost daily to find out if Pop had any animals to sell, was just on his way home and stopped in to ask how the cow was that the truck had hit. Pop told him she had died and if he would take her away he could have her to do with whatever he pleased. He thanked Pop and gave him a ten dollar bill and the butcher called his son to come with the truck to take the cow away. As Pop said later, there was really nothing more that could be done. He didn't want to undertake any legal action against the trucking company although he would write them a letter to explain what had happened to one of his best cows! As a consequence of his letter to the trucking company they did send him a twenty dollar check and apologized for the unfortunate accident which had occurred crossing the highway with our cows.

Volkmar's Return to Live on the Farm

During the years of 1940 to 1942, Volkmar spent more time with us since he no longer lived at the Hausmanns. He was living at home and attending the College of Forestry during the day as well as helping out on the farm after his studies were finished. He had discovered another student, David Caldwell, from the College of Forestry who lived in Canastota. He offered to pick Volkmar up at the farm each day to take him to the College on a daily basis. It also meant that I had the job of testing him about his knowledge of what he was studying by asking him questions about the meaning of the names of the various plants that he had to learn in his various courses. Generally, he didn't have much of a problem remembering the names of the various plants and trees when I asked him these questions.

It was also in this era that the neighbors told Pop he could graze his cows on their farms since no on was renting them and they wanted to make sure that the grass would be eaten by the cows to prevent the fields from becoming overgrown with trees and bushes. Therefore, the Donlons and the Frank May farms were open for pasture by our cows. Since so much of these farms had been hay fields with lots of alfalfa and clover in them the cows seemed to enjoy grazing on them. It was also in this period that Volkmar was getting more and more interested in farming. We even had some of our bull calves castrated since Pop thought they would not only grow faster, but would put on more weight when he would sell them after a couple of years. To my surprise these young bulls, as castrated calves, became ever more dossal and tame compared to them as adults. There was one young bull to whom I took an early interest because he didn't seem to mind at all when I got on his back and rode him around in the fields. I would mount him and when i was sent out to the pasture to round up the cows for milking in the late afternoon and drive them towards the gate to drive them across the road to the barn for milking. He actually seemed to enjoy this attention and didn't seem to mind when I climbed on his back and with my stick I would tap him on one side or the other to make sure the cows were headed towards the gate. By the time winter came along, Pop decided to sell him for beef since he had grown so heavy over the summer months on the pasture. I began to understand why farmers in Europe were able to use these animals to pull their plows, wagons and equipment around as fully domesticated farm animals. If these animals would have been as quick and responsive to the demands of their owners here in the States, I could well imagine them becoming the animal tractors which so many of the European farmers had been doing for centuries!

Getting Chickens Ready for Dinner

At least once a month Mom cooked us a chicken dinner. The prize chicken was usually a rooster, but if there wasn't one available, she chose a chicken who hadn't been producing any eggs on a regular basis. The procedure was Mom held the chicken or rooster by the head with the body draped over the chopping block while I used the axe to chop off his or her head from the body. Once the head was off the rooster or chicken, it hopped around in the yard as if he or she were trying to find their head! Needless to say, they weren't successful and after a few flops around the area where the beheading had taken place, Mom grabbed the rooster or chicken by the hind legs and carried him or her into the kitchen where she placed them in a hot water basin to pull off the feathers from the body of the rooster or hen. Once she had completed this part of the operation, she sliced open the rooster or hen and took out their intestines and washed the interior as thoroughly as possible. She also did this on their necks to retrieve the livers and lungs which she said we simply do not eat. To our amazement on one occasion, the rooster seemed to continue to fly around the yard with his head cut off and we actually had to chase after him to make sure he wouldn't inadvertently fly out into the street and be hit by a car!

Mom always did an excellent job cooking the rooster or hen for dinner. And it was rare that there was much left over after everyone at the table had had enough chicken to eat. There were usually a few bones and a bit of meat left with which to make a soup as part of the next meal, but usually little meat was left over after the initial dinner had been made and consumed.

A Vacation with a Cousin in Syracuse

When I was ten years old, my Uncle Karl and Aunt Anne asked my folks if I might come for a vacation at their home at 410 Delmar Place in Lyncourt. I would be well looked after since Pop's and Karl's aunt Dote Fischer took care of their home since both of the parents of Billy had jobs and worked everyday. Uncle Karl was my favorite uncle and I agreed it would be a good summer vacation before school started again on September 5, 1938. Both Billie and I had bicycles since I used Aunt Anne's and Billy had his own. We rode around Lyncourt extensively and visited many of Billy's friends in the area. One one occasion we heard that our cousin, Norma Kesselring, was in the hospital and Billy thought we should go and see her. He was only fourteen years old at the time, but that didn't seem to matter to him.

"We can take the city bus to the hospital. I know which buses to take. We shouldn't have any problem getting up to Crouse-Irving Hospital, Fritzle."

Aunt Dote wasn't too sure she should let us go, but Billy persuaded her he knew the way and which buses to take.

"Wir werden kinene schwirichkeiten haben, Tante. E weis welche Omnibusse wir nehmen muessen!" ("We won't have any problems, Auntie. I know which buses to take!")

And thus we were off to the hospital where Norma had been placed at her mother's direction. She had had a boy friend who had gotten her pregnant which I only learned about years later. Her mother didn't want her to have someone's baby of whom she disapproved!

DONALD F. MEGNIN

In thinking back on that occasion, I am amazed that Billy's parents approved of his plan to visit Norma. There had never been much of a connection between the two families. Aunt Bertha spent very little time visiting the rest of her family that lived in Syracuse. Perhaps once or twice a year was about the extent of her visits to the rest of her family living in Syracuse.

Norma seemed genuinely pleased to see us. She and Billy carried on an extensive conversation while I waited and listened to their conversation. I really had never been in a hospital before so that I watched carefully as the nurses came and went giving Norma something to drink in a glass. I never did find out why she was there in the first place although Billy told me, "She didn't want to keep the baby!"

One impression that I never forgot about my visits to Billy's house was the fact that he knew exactly where he would take me on our bicycles to a dead end street not far from the Lyncourt school. There, he would find "rubbers" that had been used and then discarded by the couple who had used them by throwing them out the car window.

"Why are you picking them up and washing them in the creek?" I asked.

"They're dirty and I want to make sure they're clean. I might just get a chance to use them some time so I want to make sure they aren't dirty!"

"How do you use them?" I asked. "The same ways someone else has used them. You put them over your pecker so that the girl doesn't get pregnant when you shove your pecker into her!"

I really didn't understand what he was referring to so I didn't pursue the questioning any further. I simply watched what he was doing and noting how carefully he placed them in his pocket.

Swimming in Green Lake

One of the most pleasant features of our contact with Uncle Karl was that he would take us swimming in Green Lake State Park during the summer months. In the 1930s through the 1940s it was possible to park along the roadside outside of the swimming area. It cost little or nothing and was very popular for those of us who liked to go swimming yet had little or no money to pay for the parking fee inside the park. There were trails leading from the roadside to the swimming area of the park. There were trails leading from the roadside to the swimming area of the park. We usually changed into out swim suits before we got to the park or else changed after we arrived along the roadside. It was lots of fun. After a couple of hours of swimming, we usually gathered at the lakeside along one of the benches, dried ourselves off, and climbed back into Uncle Karl's car for the ride home.

A Winter Accident

While the three of us children were off to school in Fayetteville, Pop used to go into the woods and cut down dead trees to use for firewood in our stoves in the kitchen and dining/living room. It was still towards the end of the winter season and Pop thought he would drive his model B John Deere tractor up the hillside road, cross the upper fields and down the road into the woods which the previous owners had used with their horses and wagons. The roadway down into the valley was still quite icy and as the tractor crossed the layer of ice on the road way the tractor skidded down the ice and turned sideways from the heavy steel wagon pushing the tractor so that the tractor tipped over with the wagon pushing it down the hillside. Pop was lucky to have been able to jump off the tractor just before it tipped completely over, but not before he hit his left shoulder on one of the tractor lugs as it turned over and kept on going sideways over and over again to the bottom of the hillside and ended up in the roadway below with the wagon still hooked on behind. The tractor had stopped running by the time it landed in the valley so that Pop retrieved his axe and looked over his tractor. The pipes had broken off, the gas tank had been bent and the spark plugs were broken on each side of the tractor, and the radiator had holes punched into it so that the water was pouring out of the radiator. Pop noticed his left shoulder was hurting since he felt he must have hit one of the steel lugs on the left wheel as the tractor was tipping over. He realized there was not much he could do with the tractor as it was at the bottom of the hill, broken and not running. He decided to leave it exactly as it was and walked back down the hill to the house. His shoulder was hurting even more by the time he arrived at the house. He took off his jacket and shirt and had Mom rub liniment over his shoulder before he put on his shirt and sweater again. It hurt for several days and Mom kept rubbing liniment on it daily which seemed to help ease the pain. Pop was at a loss to know what to do with his ruined tractor up in the woods. He knew it would cost him a considerable amount of money just to repair the damages that he could see on the outside of the tractor. He wasn't sure what damages had occurred inside the motor of the tractor. Since it was still winter, he decided to leave things just as they were and not bother to have someone come and take a look at the damages to the tractor. He knew it was going to cost him a considerable amount of money and he thought he would wait until winter was over before he had someone walk up the hill and into the woods to try to repair the tractor!

By the first of May, the snow had pretty much disappeared. Pop had Mom call the John Deere Agency in Cazenovia and asked to have them send out a mechanic who could determine how much damage had been done got the tractor and think of repairing it where it was in the woods. The John Deere Bitner Agency sent out a mechanic who walked with Pop up into the woods to take a look at the tractor. The mechanic looked over the tractor and listed the items that would have to be replaced before the tractor could run again. The mechanic cited the following items that would have to be replaced.

"Fred, you're going to have to replace your two exhaust pipes on the tractor. You can't use the tractor without them. Second, you're going to have to replace the two spark plugs on each side of the tractor. Third, you're going to have to have a new radiator since the one you have won't keep any water in it. Fourth, you'll probably have to have your engine checked to see if there's any damage that's been done to it by turning over and over rolling down the hill. You're a little low on oil in the engine as it stands right now, but you can probably drive it down to the barn once we get the rest of the tractor in shape to drive again. If I start today on these repairs it shouldn't take more than a day and a half."

DONALD F. MEGNIN

"All right," Pop said. "I'd like to be able to drive it back down to the barn. I've got to do some plowing yet this spring."

After walking back down the hill to the house, Frank drove back to Cazenovia and reported to Mr. Bitner what he would have to do to repair Pop's tractor.

"If he hasn't done any damage to his engine, it shouldn't take very long to fix the rest of the tractor. I should have it running by the end of the day."

And after the next day, the tractor was ready to be driven back down the hill to the barn. The oil level seemed to have kept itself within the boundaries necessary to be able to use it as if it hadn't tipped and rolled over three times before it reached the bottom of the hill. The wagon, which had been hooked up to the tractor, needed to have its right front wheel straightened so that it would turn over smoothly each time the wagon was used. Pop used a crowbar to straiten the wheel and frame so that the wheel would turn over as it should without collapsing each time the wheel turned outward to go in a different direction.

After a month, Pop's arm was once again no longer a pain to him so that he could resume his normal routine of work on the farm.

As a consequence of this experience in the woods up on the hill, when Pop hired Carly Leach to work with him on the farm, one of the first projects that they carried out was the digging out of a new road down the side of the hill in the woods so that the tractor would never have got go over the side of the road and roll down into the valley below!

They dug out the roots of the trees and leveled the road way down into the valley at roughly a thirty degree angle. We never had another accident such as the previous one in all the years that we owned that part of the woods!

It was also in the woods on the hill that Volkmar erected his first winter scene as a boy scout project. He had to cut down the limbs of hemlock trees and arrange them between two large hemlock trees in such a way that the limbs covered the entire space between these two tall hemlock trees. The arrangement had to be made in such a way that there was space beneath the limbs that covered the top of the lean to to give the effect that the space beneath the limbs was large enough to cover the entire area by the limbs which clung together as if covering the area of a small house. The intent was to give the effect of a shelter from the elements once the rain fell on the extended limbs in the winter and then froze giving the effect of an iced shelter under which persons could be sheltered from the ravishes of winter by a roof which had frozen solid as a shelter from the rest of the winter storms. So long as the ice never melted, the shelter stood as a protection against further storms under which persons could feel safe and comfortable while the winter weather raged outside. It was a truly well done experience for which he earned additional credit as a boy scout in gaining one of his many merit badges under the guidance of his Boy Scout leader, Arthur Hossbein.

Expectations Which Never Became a Reality

In thinking back over the years that Volkmar spent living and working on the farm, I was always impressed with his descriptions of what he planned to do for the future of the farm as we sat together looking over the vast display of land over which our cows wandered on farm land which was part of the Frank May farm and the Kelly farm which were no longer being worked by the owners due to the sale of the land to other owners, such as the Donlons, as the new owners of the kelly farm, and the May farm which had belonged to Frank May, one of Pop's early tutors in farming.

"What I'd like to do is buy all of these nearby farms and convert them into our dairy farm as we raise more and more cows and control all of the land from here to Mycenae and eventually the old Eire Canal," Volkmar would say. "This would be the biggest farm in this region and we could have more than five hundred cows which would make us the richest farmers in the area!"

"Do you think you would be satisfied with becoming a full time farmer?" I asked him.

"Well, why not? The only other farmers would be the big farmers this side of Chittenango and Gates Gridley, just west of Mycenae! There would be no one else who would have the same acreage that we have and we could expand our dairy into the biggest one in the area!"

Raising Different Crops

We often raised crops that Pop thought the cows would enjoy. One such occasion was in the thirties. Pop and Volkmar had loaded up the old hay wagon with the ripened crop of oats which had dried out in the hay field. Mom and I were on the load of oats and as we were going up towards the gate along the Route 5 highway, the wagon shook and seemed to disintegrate as the tractor pulled us over the rocks on the roadway leading up to the gate. All of a sudden, the front part of the wagon seemed to shake violently and Mom and I found ourselves buried under the oats which had been loaded on the wagon by Pop and Volkmar. Pop stopped the tractor and he and Volkmar dug through the oats to find us underneath the pile of oats! They dug us out and other than being covered by oat stalks, we survived very well! The wagon was no longer usable so Pop bought another one that was entirely made of steel. He and Volkmar made a wooden cover for it so that from then onward we never had a problem using our tractor-wagon combination thereafter. Pop and Volkmar succeeded in carrying the oats in the wheel barrow that day and one fork load after another was done by pitch fork spreading the oats over the hay in the hay barn. It was a slow way of getting the job done, but at least it was finished before it started to rain that evening.

An Investment in Piglets

During the thirties, Pop bought five little piglets from the farmer with whom he had become acquainted in Chittenango. He had built a pig pen behind the cow barn along the roadway leading up to the top of the hill. There was a time when the young piglets pushed their way through an opening under the rear boards on the pig pen and wandered off to the neighbors farm (Murrays) to the east. Pop followed the foot prints all the way to the neighbor's barn and when he arrived at the door of the neighbor's house, George Murray asked, "Were their footprints readable all the ways up here from your farm, Fred?"

"Yes they were. It was easy to follow them. I'm glad you let them into your barn, George. It would have been a hard job taking them back home again if you hadn't let them into your barn!"

Pop tied a rope around the neck of the male piglet and took him to the front of the rest of them and they followed him home where he put them into the pig pen again. He had already replaced the bottom board which had been pressed through by the piglets which had allowed them to escape in the first place.

The Pleasure of Riding our Horses

As a boy, we had two horses that were blind. Whenever we were going to go anywhere on the farm, Pop took me along. In fact, he thought it would be best for me to ride on Lady. The harness that she carried was similar to that of Dick and Tom except she was a vey gentle horse and Pop thought ridding on her would be the safest for me since she never reared up or became impatient with the tasks to which she was harnessed. After harnessing Dick and Lady, Pop would place me on Lady's back just behind the two knobs which were for children to use when they rode on the horses. As he set me up on Lady's back he would say, "Arschloch Hoch in America!" (Asshole high in America!) It was always a delightful ride and I always felt safe sitting on her back.

The Requirements for Building New Barns

Whenever a new section was built on the barn that Pop was in process of building, he always made sure that we placed rocks beneath the concrete which we spread over them prior to letting it harden. We drove the tractor and wagon up the hill to the field above the hillside and turned the tractor and wagon around to head back down the hill on the road which we had used to drive up the hill. At the corner just before turning down the road, we stopped at the corner and used out pick axes and shovels to dig out the rocks from the hillside. We made sure there was no dirt on them since we spread concrete over the top of them after we had placed them on the newly created dirt floor of the barn. Once we had a load of these rocks which we had dug out of the hillside, we started up the tractor and drove it down to the barn in which we were about to put in a new concrete floor. For the base of the new cow barn that we built, it took more than five wagon loads of rocks to spread over the dirt floor in order to create a hard enough barn floor surface once the concrete hardened over the rocks to maintain the kind of surface upon which the cows could stand without fear of having them fall through the cement which was then placed over the rocks. It also meant that the concrete would stay relatively warm after the cows had laid on it overnight. It seemed like an enormous job to have to do, but it was best for the cows and kept them relatively warmer in the winter when covered with straw.

After moving the saw mill down near the woods to saw up the hemlock trees into boards, two by fours, two by sixes and two by eights, Pop decided we would now clean out the fence line around the pasture on the top of the hill. There were lots of large trees such as elm, maple, hemlock and oak trees along the fence lines and on the edge of the woods. After a summer of harvesting many hundreds of trees and dragging them to the edge of the woods where Pop thought we should set up the saw mill, the anticipated job was never completed. I had been informed that Mr. Bolton (my high school friend's father) had left money for me in his will to go to college. After discussing this opportunity with Mom and Pop, they both agreed it was too good an opportunity to turn down. I therefore applied to Syracuse University and after being given a provisional acceptance, I enrolled for the fall semester and sold my tractor, two cows and Jeep to Pop and gradually left the activities on the farm to Pop and Mom. Pop only continued farming for another three years and then gave it up to assist Mom in her baking business which had developed into a wide ranging circle of customers who came regularly to buy her bread and other baked goods. Pop bought me a 1946 Ford coupe to drive back and forth to college which I used until I graduated from Syracuse.

Volkmar in High School

Volkmar was a member of the Fayetteville High School baseball team from 1935-37 as an outfielder on the Fayetteville baseball team. Over the summers, he used to play outfield for the Mycenae team when the visiting teams came to Mycenae to play our local team on the baseball field just across Route 5 in Mycenae from the Ford home. On one occasion when they were playing the Chittenango team, Volkmar hit a home run which landed beyond the outfield in the apple orchard adjacent to the playing field in grass which did not yield the ball to any of the searchers during the game nor even after the game. As the empire said, "Anything that's hit that far out is automatically a home run! We don't even have to search for it!"

Our Community Suppers

One of the real treats which we had as children was while living on the farm was attending the monthly Community Suppers also held in the Mycenae School House. Since our neighbor, Mrs. Spencer, was kind enough to take Mom and me each month, it was an opportunity to mingle with my classmates and neighbors not only enjoying the food, but also the programs which were presented by the various touring groups traveling through central New York in our area. I was only five years old but I well remember the movie presentation which one guest lecturer gave on his travels through the United States during the early nineteen thirties. Even as a boy I was impressed with the wide diversity of landscapes which the United States had and the differences between and among the various sections of the country from north to south and east to west! It was a rare treat which all of us children enjoyed and we were glad Mrs. Spencer took us along on a monthly basis. Since we didn't have a car, the kindness of our neighbor was appreciated.

The Anger of a Little Boy

I was about four years old when Herr Ernst Grossman took Volkmar, Inge and Mom up to Lake Ontario for a Sunday outing. Since I was considered too young for such a long trip, I had to stay at home with Pop. Needless to say, I was very disappointed although as Mom reminded me, I had some new kittens to play with since they were born just two weeks earlier. When Mr. Grossman drove off, I looked for the kittens and found them in the rear of the garage. I picked them up one by one and dropped them into the rain water barrel standing under the rainspout next to the back porch. Needless to say, they started a concerted effort to arouse the rest of the household to what was happening to them! Even their mother jumped up to the edge of the barrel and I pushed her into the rain barrel as well as the kittens! She started meowing and clung to the wooden barrel with her claws. The kittens tried to do the same but most of them fell back into the water. The mother cat meowed quite loudly and before I knew what was happening, Pop had come out to find out why the cat and the kittens were making such a loud noise! By the time he reached me next to the barrel, two of the kittens had drowned and were lying on the bottom of the rain barrel. The other three were hanging on to the sides of the barrel next to their mother. Pop took the three kittens and mother off the barrel and set them on the porch. The other two floated to the top of the water and he took them out and planted them in the garden. The other three ran off with their mother into the inner wall of the garage where they stayed for the rest of the day!

"Donald, weich Du was gesehen ist mit die kleine Ketzen?" ("Donald, do you know what happened to these little kittens?")

"Nein. Sie sind nicht mehr heruff gekommen!" ("No, they never came back.")

"Ja. Sie sind versoffen im Wasser! Die kleine Kettchen wissen nicht wie man schwimmt!" (Exactly! They drowned in the water! The little kittens can't swim!"

And so I found out at an early age that kittens can't swim and even an adult cat is not pleased to be pushed into a tank of cold water!

Upon Volkmar and Inge's return from their outing at Lake Ontario, they were very angry at what I had done to their cat and kittens! I stayed near Mom for the rest of the day so that they wouldn't hit me for what I had done! I was also still angry with them because they didn't take me with them!

When a Cow Wants Her Calf

Pop had bought a couple of cows on one occasion. One was an older cow and the other was a young cow just entering the age of milk production after her first calf was born. We were working on putting the second floor in the new barn when I noticed this young cow, who had given birth to a calf just two days earlier, was spending a lot of time next to the gate on the opposite side of the road. After another fifteen minutes this young cow was looking up at us in the barn as if to say, I want to see my new calf! She had jumped over the bar in the gate across the road and had walked up to the barn as if she knew exactly what she was doing. She wanted to see her calf and let her drink if she wanted to do so! I jumped off the ladder and went over to her and petted her. She seemed to enjoy the company and then moved closer to the barn door as if to say, I want to see my new calf! I opened the barn door and let her in. Her calf was overjoyed got see her and her mother came right up next to her so that she could start sucking on her teats. I watched for a short time and then Pop asked, what's the matter? "Weshalp tuts Du Sie nicht neben ihren Kalb tune Sodas das Kalb trinken kann? Deshalb ist Sie herreber gekommen!" ("Why don't you put her in the stanchion next to her calf? This is the reason she jumped over the gate!")

I did as he suggested and put some hay in front of her so that she could spend the rest of the day in the barn with her calf. Very wisely, Pop suggested that the next day we should tie her calf out in the pasture so that she would be near her calf and wouldn't attempt to jump over the gate bars anymore. This is what we did for the next few days and the mother cow gradually got used to being separated from her daughter so that by the end of the week, we no longer had to take her calf across the road. The cow was willing to stay with the other cows until we drove them all across the road at five o'clock to milk them.

The calf was gradually weaned from its mother and no longer spent more then a few minutes with her until she had had her fill of the milk from her mother. We weaned the calf from the mother by giving it access to the female goats for its breakfast and supper each day.

It was a chore to drive the cows across the busy highway twice day. There was one instance where Pop had let down the bars to the gate and the cows started moving across the highway. Pop had his back to the cars and trucks coming from the direction of Chittenango, but he did notice a large truck seemed to have trouble stopping. He got out of the driver's way but the truck still struck one of the cows. She fell over and slowly got up again with a slight limp as she made her way across the road. The driver was apologetic and said he was having trouble with his brakes not taking hold that day. Pop told him he should have stopped much earlier in order not to hit any of his cows.

"I tried," the driver said, "But my brakes had just started to weaken when I've been trying to stop."

He gave Pop his name and address and told him to contact his employer. By the time the cow had reached the gate to the barnyard, she laid down again and it was with some effort that we got her to get up again and make her way into the barn. She lay down again and had to be prodded to get up in order to milk her. When Sam, the butcher, came by that next morning, Pop sold him the cow. He didn't think she was going to last much longer. Evidently the truck had hit her harder than anyone knew. Sam barely got her to the slaughter house before she collapsed again and was unable to get up.

Protecting Our Neighbor's Heifers

Since our neighbor didn't want any Guernsey cattle mixing with his Holstein cows, Volkmar decided we should tie our bull to one of the telephone poles crossing our front lots on the north side of the road. After achieving the task of putting a ring in the bull's nose, he tied a fifty foot long rope to the ring and to one of the telephone poles crossing our front lots on the north side of the road. This worked out quite well until our cows became somewhat upset with the wind blowing up a storm. They started running across the fields and our bull decided to join them in this marathon! He started out running with them and once they got started, he obviously didn't know there were limits to what he could do. As a consequence, he ran with a group of cows and once he reached the end of his rope, he simply kept on going only to have the ring rip out of his nose. His nose was detached. Needless to say, it took some time until we were able to bring him into the barn and in a stanchion from which he was not removed until we sold him to Sam Maloff, the man who bought most of the animals which we no longer wanted to keep. It was too bad, but we had no alternative. We simply raised another young bull while using the breeding service of the veterinarian until the young bull matured enough to conduct his own affairs.

Getting Rid of Trash on the Farm

One of the discoveries that was made early by my parents was the place in which the discards of the farm were deposited. The creek, which started from underground springs of water near the outer edges of the slhucht (Valley) where the first trees had sprouted years ago and became the same depository which Pop used to deposit materials and equipment which he no longer wanted to use or had simply worn out. It was approximately fifty yards from the edge of the woods and the creek had already begun to spread out into a wider stream which then continued through the woods all the way to the northern edge of the woodlot where it flowed into the northern neighbor's creek. There were remnants of old cars (such as chassis, wheels, and roof segments), deposited by previous owners and users of the farm. They were obviously items which were not burnable and could only rust away as time would determine. Actually, the metal could have been salvaged possibly for melting, but since the remnants were of the very late 19th and early 20th centuries, it must not have been viewed as satisfactory for that period of time.

The result was that Pop dumped all of his unwanted items or junk, for which he no longer had a use, to be added to the collection which had started so many years previously. Even glass objects were dumped in the creek which Pop's brother, Karl, found and set up on nearby trees for target practice by his son and nephews when they came to visit on the farm. I often thought the glass items were dangerously unsafe for the cows that sometimes wandered into the creek but, fortunately, were never the victims of what could have been disastrous for their feet! It was a yearly ritual that during the April melting season, the tractor was hooked up to the wagon, the throw away items loaded on the wagon, and hauled down to the woods for deposit in the creek.

A Craving for the Salt Block

One of the features that I enjoyed most each spring was putting the cows out to pasture and placing a big four square block of salt out for them to lick to their hearts content. I used to take a small hammer and knocked off a piece of the salt block to put in my pocket to nibble on as the day ran on. It actually tasted quite good, I thought, after breaking pieces off to place in my mouth and chew on as the day progressed. I only did this when the block was placed out in the pasture before the cows had licked off the edges and left nothing untouched except for what was under the salt block on the ground. By then, I no longer had an appetite for what was left on the salt block!

The Use Made of a Younger Brother by an Older Sister

What an older sister requires of a younger brother is someone with whom to play and to have him substitute for a little sister which the older daughter never had! Many a time she dressed me up in the clothes of her mother and said "Now you look like our aunt!" There wasn't much I could do since she took me off to the upper stairs closet some distance away from our mother. She dressed me in high heels, dresses, and made me carry items which she said only a girl could carry! There wasn't much I could do except to become the party girl my sister insisted I had become! Actually, I must have enjoyed most of these activities. I don't recall ever complaining to our mother that I didn't like to dress up as a girl and play the part of a make believe friend of my sister. Very often she took me along when she had the assignment of taking care of the herd of goats that we had. It was on the weekends that her assignment was to let the goats out on pasture and it was her job to make sure they didn't move into a neighbor's fields to enjoy their leisure of sampling products which were not theirs to sample. She also took a book along to read and whenever some of the goats disappeared under the neighbor's fence she would yell to me, "Donald, go chase the goats out of the neighbor's yard and drive them back over here where they belong!" She would start yelling at the goats and as I made my way over to the field in which they had made themselves at home, They would start running back through the fence and into the pasture in which my sister was sitting. One feature of their pasture grazing which was difficult to curtail was their intense interest in eating apples, leaves, and items besides the grass of which they seemed to have more than they wished. We had several little stands of sumac trees, grapes, and other young trees of which the goats seemed especially fond. Whenever they were chased back from the neighbors' field, they spent the next hour or more placing their front feet against a tree or rock so that they could reach the highest leaf to consume. Usually, the goats would then break away from their pleasurable imbibing and race for the water pumps and wait until one of us would pump the tubs full of cold water for them to drink. There was a real social standard which all of the goats seemed to follow. The older, dominant, and larger goats drank first and did no allow other goats, except their young, to join in the thirst quenching effort. When one of the dominate, older ones had had enough they would allow the younger goats or non-related goats to come to the water tanks to drink.

Hierarchy Among the Cows

The social hierarchy was as stringent among the cows as it was among the goats. The older cows came to the water tanks first together with their younger heifer daughters or cows which they had produced through the years. If another cow tried to chase away one of the younger cows while their mothers were still there the cow that was trying to keep them out would be butted out of the arena by the older more dominant cow! Each animal became aware of her rights and limits according to the hierarchy which had formed in the net work of the dominate cows and which none of the newer and younger cows was allowed to break except at risk to their own safety!

The dominance was also found among the older cows as well when going from the pasture to the barn. Whenever I drove my Jeep up to the flock of cows lying down under the shelter of the trees, the leaders invariably got up first and made their way to the head of the line which they maintained all the way to the barn. None of the younger or less powerful cows would run the risk of trying to break into the line up from the fields to the barn or even from the gate to cross the road to the barn. Each cow seemed to know "her place" in the line up. If she didn't, one of the older or more powerful cows let her know by goring her with a horn or two in the hind leg so that she would move quickly out of the way and retreat to the rear of the line up! Yet each cow seemed to know exactly where she belonged in the line up and didn't break into the line up except at her own peril!

Cutting Down Cedar Trees for Our Fences

One of the projects which Volkmar and I carried out each winter was the cutting down of cedar trees and then putting them into twenty-five foot lengths for replacement on the rail fences should any broken ones need to be replaced. Since the only tractor we had in those days was a steel wheeled John Deere. It was necessary to haul these cedar lengths out of the woods by hand. With steel wheels, the snow usually clung to the steel wheels and it was impossible to drive the tractor more than ten feet before it would be necessary to knock off the snow from the front and back wheels wasting an enormous amount of time. Subsequently, Volkmar decided it was better to leave the tractor in the garage and we would saw down the cedar trees and cut them into twenty-five foot lengths before hauling them out of the woods by hand. Needless to say, we spent more time hauling the cut up cedar trees out of the woods than we did sawing them down in the first place. Since this practice had been going on for decades, we seldom had to split any of the cedar trees since they were relatively small in diameter to begin with.

An Encounter With An Angry Bull

There was a time when Pop rented the south side of the farm to our neighbor, George Murray to use for pasturing his cows on our hill top. On one occasion, Volkmar and I went up the hill to take a look at the Murray cows grazing on our hilltop pasture. As we were watching the cows from the inside of the pasture facing the open fields, George's bull came charging towards us from across the fields.

Volkmar yelled, "Donald, jump over the fence! The bull is coming towards us!"

Volk jumped on the rail fence and climbed the nearest tree. I jumped over the rail fence and as the bull was looking at me behind the fence and beginning to paw the ground, Volk yelled down from the tree, "Donald, run down the hill! The bull's going to charge right through the fence!"

I turned and ran like mad down the hill and into the house. As I came into the house, Mom asked "Was ist los? Warum bist Du so snell ins Haus gekommen?" ("What's the matter? Why have you come into the house so fast?")

Volk told me to run. He's up a tree on the top of the hill and he said Murray's bull was going to jump over the fence to get me if I stayed there!"

"Was tut Volkmar? Ist er sicher wo er ist?" ("Where is Volkmar? Is he safe where he is?")

"I think so. He's way above the bull. I don't think the bull even knows he's up in the tree!"

After another half an hour, Volkmar came into the house. He told us the bull had left to join the cows and didn't even notice him

DONALD F. MEGNIN

climbing down the tree. The next day, Pop talked to George about having his bull out with his cows.

"George, it's dangerous to have your bull out with your cows on our hill. Do you know what your bull tried to do yesterday?"

"No. What happened?"

"He ran after my two sons when they tried to see your cows on our hill!"

"Oh, I didn't know that, Fred! If I let my cows out on your pasture again, I'll keep the bull in the barn!"

"Okay. I just thought you ought to know what happened yesterday. Your bull could have caused some serious damage to my sons!"

"Thanks for telling me, Fred. If I let my cows out in your pasture again, I'll keep the bull in my barn! I didn't know he was that dangerous!"

After this one episode, we never had any other problems with Murray's bull. After all, during the thirties he as the only bull that Pop used to breed his Holstein cow. The mixture of Holstein and Guernsey produced cows that not only produced a generous quantity of enriched milk, but milk which helped Pop gain an additional amount of money for his higher test milk!

Help From the Hausmanns

It was late October when Tante Gretel and Onkel Richard came out to the farm to help Pop pick his corn crop. There was only about five acres of corn planted, but it was an abundant crop with big ears of corn sometimes as manny as three per stalk of corn. They arrived on the Syracuse-Utica Bus Line that stopped wherever a person wished to get off. After greeting Mom and Pop, Pop drove them down on the wagon to the back lot where the corn was located. The stalks were tall and whenever anyone walked in the corn rows, they were quickly lost from site. Pop told them to tear off the corn cobs and strip the cobs of their leaves so that just the bare corn was to be left in piles about twenty feet apart in every row of corn. This allowed Pop to drive the tractor and wagon through the corn rows in order to pick up the piles of corn which had been plucked from the corn stalks. After a day of diligent plucking, Tante Gretel and Onkel Richard had made many piles of corn across the field to pick up and place in his wagon. Except for the luncheon break, Tante Gretel and Onkel Richard had picked all of the corn stalks and Pop was able to pick them all up before dark.

At five o'clock that Saturday afternoon, Tante Gretel and Onkel Richard walked across the road in front of our farm house and took the bus back to downtown Syracuse where they boarded another bus for the north side of the city in order to walk the five blocks back to their home on 207 Knaul Street in Syracuse, New York. It was one of the few times that our aunt and uncle came out to the farm to help Pop harvest one of his crops. They hadn't done that since 1929 when they spent the spring and summer on the farm with Tante Gretel caring for tourists who wished to spend the night in the farm house on their way East or West on Route 5 while Onkel Richard helped Pop with the work on the farm. During that spring, their daughter, Grete, spent the time walking with Volkmar and Inge to the Mycenae School House each day to attend school. All five classes were taught by Mrs. Doer who lived in Chittenango, New York and was the sister of George Murray.

The Premier Barn Which Pop and I Built

It was in 1947-48 that Pop and I built this premier cow ban which came from the trees we cut down, pulled out of the woods and sawed into lumber which constituted the basis upon which we built this 110 foot long cow barn just to the southeast of the old farm house in which we lived. It was built upon the foundation of the blocks lying on the eastern two-thirds of the foundation which Fritz Schoeck built in the course of single Saturday in 1947. The eastern part was built in 1947 and the final second floor was completed in the spring of 1948. The picture was taken in the early 1960s when Pop had rented it to a builder who built homes in the wider Chittenango area. Since I had left the farm in 1950 to attend college, my work on the farm was limited at best and left mostly to Pop to maintain as he saw fit.

The picture is of Pop's sisters, brother and wife and brother-in-law plus Julie and me on a visit to the farm in the early nineteen sixties. Mom took the picture, so, unfortunately, she was not in the picture. This is the barn which allegedly caught fire on an early Saturday morning (2 a.m.) in the middle sixties after Pop had mentioned to the building equipment owner if he didn't start paying his rent (after five months of non-payment) he was going to have to move his operation out of Pop's barn! By the time the Chittenango Fire Department arrived, the fire had consumed so much of the barn, the department focused their attention upon saving the house, which they did. The fire destroyed the barn completely, but fortunately Pop had been able to drive the tractor and Jeep out of the western part of the barn before the building was completely destroyed.

DONALD F. MEGNIN

The upshot of the rental of the barn and loss of all of the building materials which were contained in it, simply meant Pop lost everything he had invested in the construction of the barn. The tenant simply left with no payment for the five months that he had rented the barn and Pop never thought of suing him for his months of free tenancy!

Putting in a New Water System

It was after we had built the new barn and had installed the watering system for the cows to help themselves whenever they were thirsty that we ran out of water. We had a twenty-two foot deep well which had provided the watering needs for not only our cows, but for us living in the house as well. When we noticed that the cows were not able to access the water in each of their stanchion locations because there was also no water coming out of the faucets in the kitchen and shower, Pop said we had better check on the water in the well. We opened the top of the deck on the well and placed a ladder through the opening. I climbed down into the well and on my way down I noticed things I would never have thought possible in a well from which we got our drinking water as well as for the rest of our human and animal needs. There were remains of rats caught between the rock walls of the well. There was mud several inches thick on the bottom of the well, and little if any water available although it did start to trickle in again as Pop dropped a pail and shovel down on a rope. He thought it would be a good idea to shovel the mud into the pail and he would pull it up on the rope and dump it in the garden nearby. I filled several pails full of mud for him to pull up and dump nearby. The water slowly started to flow back into the bottom of the well. When I came back up Pop and I discussed what se should do.

"Donald, sags zu Mamma Sie soll Herr Bringer anrufen und sie soll ihm sagen wir brochen einen Wasser system für unsere Kiehe. Unseren Bronnen ist Lehr!" ("Donald, tell Mom to call Mr. Bringer and tell him we need a new water system for our cows. Our well is empty!")

DONALD F. MEGNIN

I went into the house and told Mom to call the well driller that we need a new well as soon as possible. She did and he said he would be there the next morning to start drilling for a new well. He arrived at eight a.m. and set up his drill just outside of our cellar wall and began the process of drilling for water. It was only a couple of hours later when he announced "I've struck water at only forty-eight feet. You have more than forty feet of water available in your new well. I'm going to close up the operation. You don't need any more water than that!"

After the driller left, Pop told me to start digging a trench from the house to the barn and he would dig out a trench for the connection to the pump in the cellar. It took me only a day to dig the new trench from the well to the barn and after Pop finished digging the connection from the well to the pump in the cellar, we laid the pipe in both the trench to the barn and to the cellar. It took some time to connect the pipe with the water in the well and then in the cellar. It was the next day that we completed the connection with the pipes going to the barn. Once the connections were all completed, there was plenty of water for the cows in the barn and for us in the house. I covered the trench to the barn and then to the house. We then no longer had to pump the water for the cows from the well. It took me a few days to get used to the fact that there had been dead animals in the well water from which we had been drinking for years. Nevertheless, all of us had survived and the water in the well is once again full even though the new owner doesn't use it since he has access to the well next to the house which is the well we had drilled some years ago.

My Favorite Middle School Teacher

She was my fifth grade teacher at Fayetteville Elementary School. I found her to be an excellent teacher who was friendly, supportive, and helpful in every way for us to learn what she taught us in fifth grade. I was very disappointed that I had to miss several days of her class one spring due to an outbreak of measles. There was nothing I could do except wait out the outbreak which took more than two weeks to subside. She was also on duty occasionally after school to supervise conduct in the cafeteria while we waited for our school bus to arrive and take us home. We usually stayed in the cafeteria when it was raining outside and Miss Stack encouraged us to read materials she brought with her from her room. She also had the job of looking after all of us who were located in the cafeteria especially watching over those boys who had been difficult in class and were assigned to the basement after school to wait for the bus or to spend an hour of silence because of their dislike for school and causing disruptions in their classrooms. I was always dismayed by the rude behavior of some of the boys who were kept after school on detention for an hour because of their disruptive behavior in the classroom. Miss Stack seemed to handle them well even when some of the boys insisted on sitting on the floor on the tablets rather than on the benches on each side of the table. Miss Stack seemed to enjoy our company since it was such an improvement over what she had to put up with when some of the boys refused to sit on the benches and preferred to sit under the tables!

Upon graduation from high school on June 22, 1946, I was astounded to receive an envelope containing a five dollar bill from

DONALD F. MEGNIN

Miss Catherine Stack. The note read "For your success in graduating with your classmates, Donald, in spite of all of the work you had to do on your farm each spring. You deserve to be rewarded for your ability to overcome these odds and graduate with your classmates."

Needless to say, I was overwhelmed and saved the five dollar bill for more than twenty years before reluctantly spending it for fear it might not continue to be a viable currency in the distant future! Actually, my mother had continued to save it and she gave me the five dollar bill which I felt I needed after so many years had passed by. She kept the original until she died. I thanked Miss Stack for the gift after graduation, but I never wrote her a letter of thanks which I regret not having done so all of these years!

The Day the Huge Elm Tree Crashed

It was a blustery, windy day in early September when Pop and I went down to the hay field next to the Kelly field on the west side of our farm to pick up the rest of the bales which had not yet been picked up that previous day. As I was loading the bales and Pop was pilling them on the hay wagon, I looked up towards the house and noticed the large elm tree that had been standing next to the house was no longer there. It had fallen over on the eastern end of the roof of the house and extended out into the first lane of the highway. I told Pop what I saw and we both decided we better go home and see what we could do to remove the tree limbs from the road and from the eastern end of the roof of the house. I drove the tractor and wagon up to the road and left the wagon next to the gate while Pop opened the gate to let me drive through to the south side of the highway. We decided we had to remove the branches from the highway first and then remove them from the eastern rooftop of the house. Pop went into the workshop and got his two man saws and then brought them out so that we could saw off the furthest limbs extending out into the highway and drag them off the highway. There were a few cars that were passing and they slowed down. If they were driving east, they waited until no cars were coming on the highway from the eastern lane and then continued their way eastward. Once we had cut off the limbs extending out into the highway, I pulled them into our yard. I couldn't go close to the house because the huge limbs extending out towards the barn simply blocked the driveway. As soon as the branches were pulled off the highway, Pop and I got to our ladder and I climbed up to the roof of the house to see what damage had been done to it. After I climbed to the top of the roof, Pop also came up to see what damage had been done to the roof.

DONALD F. MEGNIN

"Wir müssen zuerst die aecht ab machen und dann die aecht herunter wuerfen, dann müssen wir die Dach lascher zumachen." (Well have to remove the limbs and then repair the holes in the roof.)

"Okay. I'll stay up here and cut off the limbs and throw them down so you can put them in a pile."

And that's what we did. It didn't take me very long to clear off the roof, but I did have to drive to Chittenango to Metcalfs Hardware Store and buy a few rolls of tar paper to cover the holes that were made in the roof. Fortunately for us, there was no rain that day so that we didn't have any damage done to the rooms in the eastern end of the house!

Once the roof was cleared and the tarpaper replaced with a new cover, no further damage was done to the house. The highway had also been cleared of branches so that there was no longer any danger of the drivers running into any damage to their cars or to each other. The real problem was, however, the size of the limbs extending out southward towards the barn. They were of enormous size and we didn't want to try to cut them off by using the cross-cut saw. It would have taken the rest of the day and then some.

"Mamma kann UnKol Karl anrufen und sagen Er soll seine electrise sag machine heraus bringer und die gross eachte versaegen?" ("Mom, could you call Uncle Karl and ask him to bring out his electric saw so that we can saw up these enormous logs?")

And that's what Mom did. Uncle Karl and his son, Billy, came out to the farm that next Saturday and began sawing these huge limbs into lengths that could be split and moved relatively easily. It was more than three weeks before we could use the driveway again because of the time it took to saw up these logs, split them and move them out of the way in order to use our driveway again. The ultimate result was the complete ending of the life of this huge elm tree from our front yard. Over the next two years, Pop began the process of digging into the base of the tree roots which were more from the tree and more than thirty feet in diameter just above the roots. He also poured gasoline on the stump and set it on fire which ultimately consumed the crest of the tree stump so that today there is nothing left of the tree and grass has recovered the area in which the tree once stood!

Having Fun with the Jeep

I enjoyed driving my Jeep around the countryside, I worked for the Carrier Corporation for a few months in 1947 from 3:30 p.m. to 12:30 a.m. Driving home late at night was a bit of a problem at times so I turned off my lights if there was a bright moon out that evening. Whenever there was a car coming towards me from the other side of the road, I would turn my head lights on until the car had passed. The dimming of my headlights helped to keep me awake. As soon as the car had driven past, I turned off my headlights again until the next car passed. This dimming of my headlights helped to keep me awake. As soon as the car had driven past, I turned off my headlights until the next car passed. Since I drove home on what I thought were back roads, there wouldn't be much traffic that late at night. Generally, this was the case. Instead of going home on the back roads, I occasionally travelled on the busier highway, such as Route Five. I had to turn my headlights on and off more regularly because of the increased traffic which I encountered on this road. One night, as I was driving home from work, I kept my lights off for quite some time since I hadn't encountered any cars going in my direction. After what I thought were several miles, a New York State policeman pulled me over.

"What's wrong with your lights? Why aren't they on?"

I sheepishly told him what I was doing. "I'm trying to keep awake driving home to the County line. I've noticed that I'm much more awake when I drive with my lights off than when I drive with them on!"

"That may be true for you, but it's dangerous for others who are also using this road! I'm going to have to issue you a ticket for driving

DONALD F. MEGNIN

without your lights on. You'll have to see Judge Gridley tomorrow since I'm giving him a copy of the ticket I'm issuing you! Do you know where he lives?"

"Yes. I've known him for a long time."

"I want you to keep your lights on and I'm going to follow you to make sure that you do. We can't take any chances like this on a busy highway even if you are tired!"

He wrote up the ticket and gave it to me to take to Mr. Gridley that next day. When I arrived home, I wrote a short note to Mom to tell her to be sure to wake me up early because I had received a traffic ticket last night for driving without my lights on!

Sure enough, Mom woke me up at eight o'clock. I usually slept until nine or even ten o'clock in the morning, depending upon what Pop had planned for me to do on the farm before going off to work at Carrier in the afternoon.

"Was ist mit Dir passiert gestern Abend das Du stumm Herr Gridley gehen muss heute?" (What is it you have to do today because of what you did yesterday? Warum muss Du Herr Gridley heute besuchen?"

("I was getting sleepy and decided to drive with my lights off last night. The moon was really bright so I had plenty of light by which to see where I was going!")

"Aber der Polizist hat es nicht geglaubt." ("But the policeman didn't believe it.")

"I've done this quite often. This was simply the first time that I got caught! It was a really bright moonlit night. If the policeman hadn't come up behind me I wouldn't have been caught!"

"Und jetzt muss Du zum Gericht gehen und wahrscheinlich eine Bestrafung bezahlen." ("And now you have to go before the judge and probably pay a fine.")

("I don't know. If Pop goes with me I think maybe Mr. Gridley will only give me a warning.")

Das muss Du mit dem Papa aus machen. Er weist noch nichts von dessen Bestrafung vom Polizei." ("You'll have to work that out with your father. He knows nothing about the fine from the police.")

GROWING UP ON A FARM

After I are my breakfast, I went out to the barn and told Pop what had happened. He listened and then said, "Wir werden spater zum Herr Gridley fahren und ausfinden wievie diesen ticket kosten Wirt." ("We'll go up to the Gridley farm later and find out what the cost of the fine is.")

Later that morning, I drove us up to the Gridley farm and we talked with Mr. Gridley about my ticket.

"How did you happen to receive this ticket from the trooper, Donald?"

I explained to him that quite often I get very sleepy driving home late at night.

"When I turn my lights out, I pay much better attention to the road, Mr. Gridley. It was a full moon last night and there was plenty of light by which to see what was in the road."

"Yes, but you know that after dark you have to use your head lights, right?" "Yes, I know that. It's just that I've noticed if I turn off my headlights at night with a bright moon, I can see very well what's ahead of me on the road."

"Fred, you understand what I'm trying to tell your son, don't you? It's against the law to drive with your lights off at night no matter how bright the moon shines!"

"Yes, I understand, Mr. Gridley. I'm sure he won't do it again."

"Swell, I certainly hope not, for his sake. He could lose his license if this happens again, Fred."

"I understand, Mr. Gridley. What does he have to pay for breaking the law while driving without his lights on?"

"I'm going to forgive him this time, but if it happens again, I'll have to revoke his driver's license. Do you understand, Donald?"

"Yes, I understand. Thank you very much Mr. Gridley. It won't happen again."

"Well I certainly hope not in your case, Donald. But let this be a warning to you. When it's dark, leave your car lights on as you drive down a public road!"

Pop and I thanked Mr. Gridley for his generosity and left promising not to bother him again over such a situation again!

My Spring Farm Work

Working on the farm during my spring break from school attendance, I often had the job of early plowing in preparation for the planting of the summer crops. As I plowed the back lot, I often stopped and went down to the creek in the valley between the pasture around the huge tulip tree and the creek. It was the creek to which I wandered and looked for some nearby straws in an area in which the water bubbled up from the ground. This was the safest water to drink since the cows wandered through the creek in drinking as much water as they wanted. I looked for some useful straws through which I could siphon the water from these bubbling areas of fresh water arising from the depths below the creek itself. This water was fresh, clean, and cold since it came right out of the ground untouched by the cows wandering through the creek as they drank as much water as they wanted. It was an excellent way of satisfying my thirst and safe from any contamination since it came directly up from the ground. With these periodic breaks from work in order to drink some fresh water, I had no trouble working for the rest of the day heading home to help milk the cows.

Since I had to do the plowing, disking, and dragging of the fields in which Pop wanted to plant various crops each spring of the year, I had no watch, with which to tell time. I simply kept my eyes on the distant highway late each afternoon in order to see the school bus come down the highway and always turned around in our yard each afternoon after four fifteen. This would be my signal to get ready to drive the tractor back up to the barn and get ready to drive the cows back across the road to the barn for milking. Since Pop was working in Syracuse during the war producing parts for American tanks, Mom and I had to drive the cows across the road late each afternoon around five o'clock. I had the job of driving the cows through the gate unto the road while she stood on the highway and held up the red flags to stop the cars and trucks from continuing until the cows were off the road. We then started milking the cows and by five-thirty. Pop had returned from work on the bus and came into the barn to help us milk the cows. It was a slow process, but by six o'clock we were usually finished. Mom went into the house to begin cooking supper and Pop and I let the cows out on the hillside pasture after making sure they had had enough water to drink before they wandered up the hill to the pasture. It meant either he or I had the job of pumping the water from the well so that the cows had enough to drink before setting off on their journey up the hill. The pasture lots were on top of the hill and along the line of apple trees that had apples falling on our hillside lots from our apple trees and those of our neighbors.

We also had to look after the goats to make sure they had had enough water to drink and hay to eat before we retreated to the house for supper.

On occasions Pop undertook what I simply couldn't stand was the butchering of the dominant pig that we had in our pig pen. It was Helper whom I admired because he was so helpful in getting the female pigs into the shed each day when we closed them in for the night. We simply did not want them to get out, which they had done earlier in the years of their occupancy of the pig pen. Pop led Helper down to the hay barn where he attached two ropes to his hind legs and then told me to drive the tractor forward. As I did, the ropes tightened on the hind legs of Helper and pulled him up the wall of the hay barn and he started screaming as only a frightened pig can do! After I pulled him about five feet above the ground, Pop stuck a knife in his throat and the blood came gushing out. Pop had placed a big tub underneath Helper so that his blood poured into it. He kept screaming and I told Pop, "I can't take it anymore! I'm going into the house so that I won't be able to hear him anymore!"

DONALD F. MEGNIN

    I left and after about twenty minutes enough blood had drained out of Helper he couldn't cry anymore. I came to the back door of the house and not hearing him screaming anymore, helped Pop carry the container of blood into the back room of the house. Pop then returned to Helper and continued his job of taking out his intestines. His next job was to remove all of the outer hairs from his body so that he could carve him up into the regular size pieces to place in the ice box into which he could keep the meat fresh and cold and keep from spoiling. By late afternoon, Pop had completed his job of carving up Helper into the appropriate pieces to place in the refrigerator for the winter. Mom had to cook the blood so that it wouldn't spoil and make sure the rest of the meat was placed in the appropriate places among the various levels of the ice box for safe keeping throughout the year. We had enough meant for the next year. We simply had to make sure we also had enough ice available to keep the pork from spoiling should we not have enough ice in the months ahead. To her credit, Mom kept watch over the ice throughout the year and subsequently, none of the meat spoiled. It was the last time I ever helped slaughter a pig! I could weld an axe with which to prepare a chicken or a rooster for Mom to prepare for a Sunday dinner, but I could not face the death of another animal with which I had become so fond ever again!

Spreading Lime

It was a windy fall day when Pop decided, "Heute kanst Du diesen Lime vertailen über das Feld oben beim Wald." ("Today, you can spread the lime over the field on the hill next to the woods.")

Pop had ordered enough lime from the dealer in Chittenango Station to spread over all of the hay and pasture fields we had on the farm before winter set in. I loaded up the back of the Jeep and hitched the spreader to the tail gate of the Jeep and drove up the hill road to the fields adjacent to the woodlot. I loaded the sacks of lime into the spreader and began the process of driving from the woods to the lot on top of the hill back and forth. By the time I had reached the further side of the fields, an old friend of mine had come to pay a visit. It was Bob Bolton from DeWitt with whom I had begun to spend a lot of Sundays visiting not only the DeWitt Community Church, but often as his guest for dinner with his parents. It was always an enjoyable way to spend an afternoon and Bob occasionally came out to the farm to participate with me in whatever I was doing. Since he had walked up the hill to find out where I was and saw what I was doing, I stopped and told him to jump into the Jeep.

"Bob, whenever the spreader is near the end of its load, could you put in another bag or two of lime so that I can continue to finish the field before dark?"

"Yeah, I guess I could do that!"

He opened another bag of lime and poured it into the spreader. I kept on driving up and down the field as the lime came through the spreader. Needless to say, every time Bob poured in another bag of lime, the wind covered him with almost as much lime as came through the spreader unto the field! After making the trip back and forth numerous times, we finished liming the field. He was almost as white in the face and on his clothes as we had spread on the fields!

"Thanks for you help, Bob! Sorry about all of the lime that's gotten all over you, but that's one of the risks we run doing this kind of work."

"Yeah, now you tell me! I'm going to have to go home and take a shower! I can't go anywhere looking like this!"

I laughed, "Yeah, you're right! I should have told you before you offered to help how covered with lime you were going to become!"

I drove the Jeep and spreader back down the road to the barn. Bob brushed himself off as best he could and said good bye.

"I'll see you this next Sunday, if I can every get this lime off of me!"

"Thanks for your help, Bob. It's too bad you didn't come earlier. I wouldn't have had to do all of that work if you had come at the beginning of the lime spreading!"

"Thanks! It's going to take me some time to clean up the car when I get home. My folks won't want to ride in it looking as white as it will from me sitting in it!"

How Nicknames Get Started

Since we drove the cows across the highway twice a day so that they could pasture on the north side and south side of Route 5, we often had a bull with them for breeding purposes. On one occasion a classmate of Volkmar had come to pay him a visit after the day in the high school had ended. We were driving the cows and bull across the road when the bull mounted the cow he had been chasing all day. As he was crossing the gate rails, he mounted the cow and gave her a full thrust of his penis into her vagina. I was to the rear of the line of cows crossing the road and yelled out, "He got her!"

After that incident, Earl Rasmussen never forgot what I had yelled out. Every time he saw me he asked, "Fritz, did he get her?" Since we always rode the school bus together, he asked me everyday, "Fritz, did he get her?"

Needless to say. the other students always asked to what Earl was referring. He always said, "Let Fritz answer that!" It was only after Volkmar and Earl graduated from high school that the tease ended every time Earl saw me!

Baseball in Mycenae

In the summers, the field had been the Mycenae baseball field and diamond. It was owned by the Robert Ford family just across the street from their house at the three corners of Route 5 and 290 coming up to Route 5 from the Green Lake area. Since the field had not been used as a ball field the previous summer, Mr. Ford asked Pop if he'd like to cut the alfalfa and timothy off the field and store it in our barn for winter. Pop had me drive him down to look at it and then we stopped over at the Ford house and Pop said he'd be glad to take it. The next day I drove the Model A John Deere tractor and mower down to the field and mowed it and then had it baled by the Naymek Brothers that same afternoon. It proved to be a wise move since we had four big loads of bales to stack in our barn for the cows that coming winter. It also meant the boys of Mycenae could use the field for baseball practice after the hay was removed and the bases relocated where they had previously been taken off in order for the field to be mowed and harvested.

Since the baseball diamond was waiting to be mowed that summer, the boys of Mycenae had to make do with other fields if they could use them. Since the Holtz family had moved from Kirkville to Mycenae, Dale asked Roy if we might be able to use part of his pasture next to the Brady farm as a baseball diamond for a game or two before he and the other men had to return to the Army for their military service during World War II. Roy approved of the area and we played a game on the improvised lot in the corner of Roy's pasture next to the Brady lot just off the Green Lake Road. It proved to be an ideal location where the boys and young men from Mycenae could play baseball before entering the service and playing baseball which would not be played again until after the war. The cows wandered over to where we were and stood nearby and seemed to watch what we were doing. Fortunately for the cows, they simply stayed in the out field and did not mingle with any of the players even though they certainly seemed interested in what we doing! Since the war drafted all of the eligible men, we no longer had any baseball games until after the war ended and the hayfield that Pop had used previously was now once again used for baseball games only.

As boys, Volkmar and I used to play baseball using the house as the backstop for any stray balls that weren't hit or that were outside of the strike zone for us as batters. We each had thee outs per inning and because Volkmar was eight years older than I, he had to bat left handed. Even so he usually hit the ball well into the barnyard or garden so that I had a hard time running after the ball so that he had run the three bases long before I had retrieved the ball. As a consequence, he gave me six outs rather then three outs per game. On occasion, I hit the ball over the garden fence so that he had to run through the gate leading into the garden and I could sometimes beat him home by the time he had retrieved the ball. A much better game was simply hitting the ball to him for fielding practice. I preferred this since I usually had to run after the ball which he hit over the fence into the barn yard and I'd have a hard time going through the fence to retrieve the ball. Another of the games we played was to throw the ball up on the roof of the barn and catch it as it came down. It was good practice and it certainly improved my ability to catch the ball when he threw it towards the end of the barn roof and I had to run to catch it before it fell to the ground!

Things for Kids to Do on the Farm

One of the chores we all enjoyed as children was going berry picking in the fields each summer. There were black berries, strawberries, elderberries, and nuts to gather as they ripened. I must admit, I usually had more than a basket full of a variety of berries to take home while Inge and I had contributed perhaps a quart basket or two to the grand total that Mom had picked! She then made jam out of this contribution and we enjoyed eating the cooked berries that were spread over our sandwiches after lunch or supper. The best way to safeguard the source of our berry picking operations was to make sure we got to the fields before the cows did otherwise they were crushed from the cows grazing through the berry patches that were growing in odd parts of the pasture fields. Wisely, Pop kept the cows out of the best berry fields until after we had picked them pretty thoroughly.

Volk liked to go hunting each fall season. He asked me to go along with him in case he shot something. I was designated as the game bearer which meant I had to carry whatever it was that he shot. It usually meant we walked long distances and had few if any prey to carry home of something he might have shot! There was one occasion when he shot a cock pheasant one day before the season opened. Since I was rather small, he didn't want me to carry it since it would be too obvious what he had shot. He opened his jacket and placed the pheasant under his jacket. The only problem was that the tail feathers stuck out from the bottom of his jacket. I reminded him of the fact as we started to go across the road to the house. He thrust the pheasant up higher in and still the very tip of the tail stuck out under his jacket. He simple kept his hands over the end of the tail holding on to his shotgun. When he got it in the house, he cleaned the pheasant and Mom cooked if for supper that evening.

Volkmar's Return to the Farm

When Pop and Volkmar bought a couple of cows in early 1946, they thought they had bought two that would add to their milk production, which they did. However, the Holstein heifer from the earlier herd of cows before the barn fires thought she alone was in charge of the water tanks which Pop and Volkmar pumped full each morning for the cows to drink. Little did the Holstein know how strong the newcomer to the herd was. When the Holstein was drinking at one of the washing machine tubs, the huge Ayrshire/Guernsey came up behind her and nudged her in the back as if to say, okay, now it's my turn. The Holstein turned quickly towards the new cow and started to push her away from the water tank. Little did she know that the big new cow was even stronger then she and pushed her away from the water tank where she had been drinking. After being pushed back away from the water tank, the Holstein recognized she was not the stronger of the two and turned away and let the Ayrshire drink whatever amount she wanted. It was the last time that the Holstein tried to demonstrate that she was the strongest of the cows. She actually was the strongest except for this new addition to the herd. The only damage which had been done to the new cow was that her right horn was almost torn off and after a few days simply fell off the cow's head. Therefore, the Ayrshire simple wandered up to the water tanks and the other cows simply gave way so that she could drink to her heart's content. No other cow was going to try to challenge her right to drink water whenever she thought she wanted a drink! Whenever the Holstein saw her coming, she simply moved out of the way. She never again challenged her. There was no other cow that she couldn't defeat and control in the barn yard or pasture. It was only the new Ayrshire that she couldn't control.

Buying My First Bicycle

During the early 1940s, I had saved enough money to buy myself a bicycle. Since we didn't have a car, our neighbor, Mrs. Jo Parks, offered to bring the bicycle home for me in the back of her car. It was a delightful way to ride back and forth between the farm and my various friends in Mycenae. I also rode it over to Green Lake to go swimming one late afternoon. I didn't have a lock for it so I left it next to a bench along the lakefront thinking it would be safe until I was ready to ride it home. After I was through swimming, I went back to the bench where I had left my bicycle and found it was no longer there! Someone had simply ridden off on it while I was swimming in the lake! Needless to say, my parents were not pleased with what had happened! And they were in no way willing to have me buy one at their cost!

Prior to this time when I had purchased my own bicycle, our uncle Karl and Maria Fleckhammer had bought Inge a bicycle with small wheels, but it had a seat on it and she could ride it on and off to Green Lake State Park along the side of the road. She would ride ahead of me and then wait until I had caught up with her before continuing to pedal to the next stop. It took some time to reach the park, but at least we got there and kept the bicycle in sight at all times while we were in the water. After swimming for an hour or two, we would get out of the water, dry ourselves off and Inge would ride ahead and wait until I had walked up to where she was parked. By the time we got home we were usually hot and sweaty but at least we had spent some time in the water!

My Earliest Farm Work

From the years of 1942 until 1945, it was my job, especially after I had been given the privilege to drop out of school each spring from March 1st to work on the farm by my Principal, Mr. Raymond Van Giesen, to spread the enormous pile of cow manure which had been piled up outside of the cow barn each winter over the various fields scheduled for plowing and planting that spring. The manure pile was the result of wheeling it out from the cow barn each morning in a wheelbarrow and dumping it on top of the continuously growing pile added each day. The length of the pile was approximately thirty feet long by ten feet wide and five or more feet high! Pop decided it was too risky to try to use the John Deere model BR in the snow since the snow often stuck to the wheels especially after it began to warm up a bit and, with the fenders over the wheels, it simply wouldn't allow the tractor to move once the snow packed between the steel wheels and fenders! Hence, the mountainous piles of manure which had to be taken out of the cow barn on a daily basis. It was usually early May before I could then load this enormous pile of manure on the manure wagon and drive the tractor down to the fields to spread the manure over the fields to be plowed as soon as the manure had been spread! It generally took me three weeks to load, spread and continue to drive down to the various fields destined to be plowed and planted in some kind of crop for the summer. After the manure was spread, it was then my job to plow the fields, harrow and drag them so that the fields were ready for Pop to plant on the weekends when he wasn't working in the factory in Syracuse. Since we didn't have a grain drill, he had to spread the seed by hand after which I would

DONALD F. MEGNIN

then drag the field in order to cover the seeds so that they could grow into a crop to be harvested by a combine. After the grain matured, it was harvested by our neighbors' combines. Of all of the jobs I had to do on the farm, spreading the manure each spring, I considered the worst job I ever had to do on the farm! Not because it was difficult, but simply because it had to be done and I was the only one there to do it! It was only in the spring of 1945 that I was able to relinquish this ornery task. Pop had quit his job in the factory as a tool maker in January of that year since he had paid off the mortgage of ownership of the farm!

My First Real Farming Test

It was in the spring of 1943 that Pop told me to plow the back part of the field just across the road from the house. The lot was at the end of the field and Pop thought it would be a good field in which to plant oats and clover. It was early May when I started plowing the field after I had spread all of the manure. I plowed it with the John Deere model BR tractor and was doing well going from one side of the field (east and west). I noticed there was an abundance of water on the western side of the field just inside our field adjacent to the Kelly field right next door. In fact, there seemed to be water running north towards the pasture which led down to the creek through the wooded valley to the north of the farm. I kept going from east to west each time plowing more and more of the field. What I also noticed was the fact that each time I turned the tractor from west to the east, I seemed to be sinking deeper and deeper into the water. After plowing approximately two acres of this part of the field, I wanted to turn from the westside and plow towards the east. I succeeded but noticed the water seemed to be getting deeper and deeper each time I turned from west to east. As I turned around from the east and was plowing towards the west, I suddenly didn't seem to be moving anymore! My wheels were simply spinning since the bottom of the tractor was apparently hung up, on top of the previous furrow! I shifted to a lower gear and nothing changed. I was still hung up on the previous furrow! I got off the tractor and looked under the tractor to see the center of the chassis was sitting on top of an island surrounded by water. I tried to unhook the tractor from the plow but there was still no difference from what had been the case earlier. I was still stranded with the tractor sitting

DONALD F. MEGNIN

on an island of land surrounded by water. I decided I really couldn't do anything until I could lower the tractor to the ground in order to gain traction for the rear wheels. Since I did not have a shovel with me, I shut off the tractor and walked up to the workshop and got a shovel to try to dig my way out of the mud hole into which I seemed to have fallen. I started to dig under the tractor only to find that the more I dug, the higher the tractor seemed to be sitting in the water! I dug all around the sides of the tractor and tried to dig under the tractor as well. It took me all afternoon to keep digging only to find that the tractor was still hung up by the island of land under the main chassis of the tractor. By the time it was necessary to return home to milk the cows, I had tried everything that I thought might work and nothing had! I was stuck even higher than previously upon the mound of earth under the main body of the tractor. The explanation was due to the fact that I had plowed back and forth across the field so that the remaining unplowed land was what remained after I had plowed the field back and forth and each time I sliced off another sixteen inches of plowed land with the remainder left as a mound from one side of the field to the other. In other words, what had been a three acre field to be plowed was now only fourteen inches across so that when the tractor started across the remaining section to be plowed, the wheel simply returned via the plowed strip on each side of the remainder which meant the tractor drove on top of the center strip and sat there unable to move because the rear wheels simply spun around without touching the plowed furrow. The tractor was marooned on the residue of what was left of the unplowed ground between each side of the field which had already been plowed! I got off the tractor and looked around to see what I might do to correct the situation. Since I had neither a shovel nor even a rake with which to try to remove myself from the middle of the remaining furrow, I shut off the tractor and walked up to the workshop to get a shovel and a pickax with which to remove the tractor from the mound of earth upon which it was stuck. I started to dig after I told Mom what I was about to do before returning to the field where the tractor sat.

"E sags denn Papa wenn er heim kommt." ("I'll tell your Dad when he comes home.")

"Okay Mom. I'm going back down to the tractor to see what I can do to get it off the center mound of dirt upon which it's sitting."

I walked down to the field where the tractor was sitting in the mud. There had also been water in the ditch right next to the field where I was plowing. It had begun to leek into each side of the tractor wheels so that they were soon covered in mud along the bottom of the wheel. I had worn my boots down to the field since the water was getting deeper around the tractor and I didn't want to get my shoes wet. Before I left Mom said. "E sags zum Papa wenn er heim kommt. Wir werden dann ein besinn spaetter Milken als gewoehlich." ("I'll tell Papa when he comes home. We'll be milking a bit later than usual.")

"Okay. The only way I'm going to be able to get the tractor out is by digging under the main part of the tractor so that the wheels have traction in the dirt again."

And with these parting words, I made my way back down to the field in hopes of getting the tractor out before dark. As I was digging away at the dirt under the tractor, Pop came down to where I was working. We greeted each other and he looked over the situation.

"Ja Du tust es richtig, aber Du wirst es nicht fertig machen eh es Dunkl wird. Komm Heim mit Meer. Du kannst es Morgen fertig machen." ("You're doing it right. You won't finish it before it gets too dark. Come on home with me. You can finish it tomorrow.") And so we went home and I helped milk the cows before supper.

The next day I returned to the tractor that was still sitting on top of the earth mound and began digging away at the dirt. After a couple of hours, I had one wheel of the tractor on the ground again and was working on the other side. After another hour, I was able to lower that side of the tractor down to the solid ground again. I then started up the tractor and since I had unhitched the plow, I could drive the tractor out of the hole without any problem. I then backed the tractor up to the plow on the side and pulled it out of the plowed area. I then returned to the area in the middle of the plowed field and completed plowing the center strip without getting hung up again. While I enjoyed plowing fields I never again allowed myself to get hung up with the tractor on any area that hadn't been plowed! It was a hard task to learn, but I can truly say, I learned my lesson! I dragged the plowed field and disked it so that Pop could distribute the seed before I dragged it again. It was the last time I ever got stuck with a tractor in a situation that I had created myself!

My First Vehicle

It was shortly after Volkmar and Eva and their boys moved back to Minnesota that Pop suggested we go look to buy a Jeep. The four wheel drive appealed to Pop since it could be driven almost anywhere and not get stuck. We went to the same dealer that Volkmar used when he bought his Jeep in December of 1945. The dealer had several and the one that appealed to us the most was a blue Jeep which I bought and Pop cosigned to satisfy the owner of the car agency since I was Pop's employee. We also bought a three hundred pound weight to put on the bumper of the Jeep which the dealer strongly suggested since we told him we were going to use it as a tractor on the farm as well as a road vehicle. While I used the Jeep to drive back and forth to work during my months working at the Carrier Corporation, we also used it extensively around the farm not only pulling wagons, but driving down to the woodlot to cut down the trees until, with Pop's signature, I also bought a new rubber tired John Deere tractor Model A for use on the farm especially to run the saw mill. As I mentioned earlier, Volkmar and Pop found out the John Deere model BR was not strong enough to run the sawmill in the spring of 1942. After Volkmar entered the Army on August 1, 1942, Pop decided a heavier and more powerful John Deere would be able to power the sawmill. After we set up the sawmill down by the woodlot on the west hillside across from the creek, we tried the tractor on the sawmill and it certainly demonstrated it was powerful enough to supply the power for the sawmill to saw up any size log we wanted to try to saw. It was at this point that we started using the Model A John Deere to power our machinery when it was necessary to be used. I had to pay seventy dollars a month to cover the purchase cost of the tractor and Pop usually gave me twenty dollars more per month so that I might have some money available to go out with my friends on weekends. I also drove Mom down to Chittenango each Saturday to buy the weekly supply of food from the grocery store owned by the German Meyer family whose father and his twin sons owned and operated it.

Building A Bigger Barn

During the spring of 1947, Pop decided this was the time to build a bigger cow barn. He told me we were going to remove all of the mud from the barn yard, lay the foundation for the walls, and get his son-in-law (Fritz Schoeck who was a trained brick and block layer) to lay the stone blocks on the three sides of the new building. Fritz had learned masonry in Austria before emigrating to the United States in the spring of 1939. The removal of the mud and rocks from the barnyard was by far the most difficult. It took us almost a week before we had cleared out the barn yard and Pop and I dug the lines for the walls of the barn to a depth of three feet. He wanted to make sure we were down below the frost line before starting to construct the walls of the new barn. We shoveled the mud into piles next to the outer fence line which we would move out to the fields later to be plowed under as if it were fertilizer after we were through building the foundation of the new barn. I had the job of making sure Fritz had enough mortar with which to lay the blocks around the three quarters of the foundation abutting the part of the barn which Pop and Carly Leach had built in the nineteen thirties. It actually took only one Saturday for Fritz to lay all of the blocks for the new foundation of this additional cow barn for the coming winter. The next task was for Pop and and me to put on the second floor of the barn which we proceeded to do in the next couple of weeks. It also meant we had to cover the wooden floor with tar paper since it was going to have to withstand the snowfall of the oncoming winter. It was only in the next year that we would have sawed down the trees for the building of the second floor and roof of the next barn and sawed them into two by fours, sixes, and boards for the completion of the roof and second floor of the new barn. It was with pleasure that we completed building this barn. At long last, since 1932, we hadn't had as large a barn as this one and now it could hold all of the hay we could cut and put into the barn and it proved even more than enough for all of the cows and heifers we had now under one roof. Even Volkmar came on occasion to help us build the remaining parts of the new barn when he felt he had time to do so.

And A New Life Began

It was during the spring of 1950 that Mrs. Bolton and her son, Bob, told me that Mr. Bolton had left money in his will for me to go to college. He had died that spring and after discussing the opportunity with Pop and Mom they were in agreement that such an opportunity should not go unused. Pop decided to continue to farm for a few more years even though he was now in his seventies. He bought my cows, Jeep, tractor and bought me a 1946 Ford coupe with which to drive to Syracuse University each day. I helped occasionally on the farm when I could although it was not expected of me to do so.

"Wenn Du Zeit hast kanns Du immer uns helfen, aber deinen Studium ist immer voraus." ("When you have time you can help us any time, but your studies always come first.")

"Thanks, I'll remember that, Pop. What you've done for me is a big help towards achieving my goal of graduating from college!"

In retrospect one of the features of what I did two summers later is one that I've learned to regret. I had completed my second year at Syracuse University when Bob Lindeman asked me if I'd like to spend the summer working with the U. S. Forest Service in Montana. He had been doing so for a couple of years and Phil Resch, from DeWitt, had agreed to do so that next summer. Instead of talking it over with my parents, I said yes and left with Phil and Bob for Montana just when Pop was harvesting his first cutting of hay that May. Needless to say, Pop was not pleased with my decision! He refused to shake hands with me after Phil and Bob had driven down to the farm from DeWitt to pick me up for the drive out to Montana! It did prove to be an interesting experience for me since I spent most

DONALD F. MEGNIN

of the summer on a lookout scouring the horizon for forest fires while also writing short stories and articles of interest in the times between scouting the landscape every half hour for possible forest fires. Fortunately for all of us in the Forest Service that summer, we did not have any major forest fires with which to contend during my two months on the Camel's Hump Lookout that summer. During the previous month's working in cutting trails and cleaning brush from roadways and trails, we did have a trial test in trying to locate a forest fire in the National Forest as a test of our ability to locate and put out the beginning of a forest fire. I was given the location of the fire and proceeded to try to find it. I spent all afternoon and into the evening trying to locate what was presumably the beginning of a forest fire. Needless to say, I didn't locate the fire but did traverse more than twenty-seven miles in my hunt for it. I did locate the fire fighters in the nearby district and they called my Ranger District Office to indicate whom they had found at their doorstep. Since Bob Lindeman was the person in charge of our District's Office, he not only received the call, but volunteered to come and pick me up so that I wouldn't have to walk back in the dark to our Ranger Station!

An Introduction to the Ministry

As I began my junior year of college, Dr. Alex Carmichel, the minister in charge of the DeWitt Community Church, asked me if I might be interested in working twenty hours a week calling on people attending the church, but who were not members. I would be paid twenty dollars per week and I could also teach a class of high school boys Sunday mornings before the Church Service started. I agreed and began the first stages of entering the ministry program which I gradually had taken an interest in since starting to attend the DeWitt Community Church the year after I had first heard Alex preach at our high school Baccalaurate Serice in 1946. I had begun to attend his church, thanks to the invitation of Bob Bolton, who was a high school classmate of mine and a member of the DeWitt Community Church, with his father and mother. I found this experience interesting and gave me an opportunity to begin to think about what kind of a future I might choose for my life's work. I had the use of the book which each of the boys had for our weekly discussions. I found these discussions interesting and even some of the boys seemed to enjoy discussing some of the basic concepts of the Christian Faith at our weekly meetings. I was also often asked by Bob Bolton to come to their house after church for dinner with him and his parents. I found our discussions of great interest and I often took the opposite side of the discussion which I had with Mr. Bolton. He seemed to enjoy our discussions even when we were on the opposite sides of the issues as we understood them. He was very tolerant and often joked about our differences as if we had come from a different part of the world

(which I told him we had since I came from a German background and he from an English background.)

My contacts with new visitors to the DeWitt Community Church were also enjoyable even though I wasn't really a member of the Church. Probably the most enjoyable part of this church activity was the weekly meeting of the College Club which took place each Sunday evening at seven o'clock in Alex's office. Each person had an opportunity to raise an issue which we would discuss at some length among us. Usually by nine o'clock we would have discussed the issue long enough and we would go home promising to continue where we had left off that next week!

The Winter of 1947-48

It was a long, cold winter in 1947-48. Pop decided we would drive down to the woods and begin cutting down hemlock trees in order for us to saw up the logs into two by fours, two by sixes, two by eights and one inch thick boards in order to build a bigger cow barn. Volkmar and Pop had built on an edition to the rear of the cow barn and under the old silo in 1946, but there was limited room for any expansion in the number of cows that could be put into it. Pop decided we would saw down many hemlock trees that we had in the western most part of the woodlot next to the Farrell farm. I drove the Jeep with Pop down to the backlot and woods each morning after milking the cows, eating breakfast, and loading the cross-cut saws into the back of the Jeep plus the sledge hammer, wedges and axes. With four wheel drive, we had little trouble driving through the snow that winter. I deliberately stayed away from the fence lines where the snow had drifted realizing we would get stuck were I to drive too closely to the rail fences. After spending the winter cutting down the hemlock trees, we had quite a pile of logs to haul out of the woods. We used the John Deere BR tractor with a long winding cable to attach to the logs and I would pull the logs through the creek and mud just to the outside of the woodlot on the crest of the hill in front of the woodlot to the west of the creek and swamp. Pop decided to set up the sawmill on the brow of the hill just in front of the woodlot road through which I drove the tractor pulling the logs out of the woods one by one. I also had purchased a new John Deere Model A tractor to not only run the saw mill, but to use for more powerful capabilities should they be necessary around the farm. I had gone to Chittenango State Bank to take out a loan and it was approved since my parents were cosigners should I be unable to pay the seventy dollars per month loan which I had taken out to buy the tractor. By the time the snow had melted and the crops planted, Pop and I turned our attention to setting up the sawmill and making sure the tractor was aligned to run the sawmill.

We had a sizable pile of logs next to the sawmill and had placed two ironwood five inch logs from the bottom of the log pile to the sawmill in order to roll the logs up on the sawmill. We tried this system out with a small hemlock log and were pleased with the result. Not only was the tractor powerful enough to run the sawmill, but the resulting boards were a pleasure to take off as they were sawed through the log. I caught each board and set it aside on a nearby pile of boards about ten feet wide and more than twelve feet in length. As each log was sawed into boards, Pop also made sure we sawed the logs into two by fours, sixes, eights and twelves as he determined they would be needed in building a new cow barn after completing the sawing up of the logs. It should be mentioned, it took us some time to complete the pulling out of the logs from the woods. We used a seventy five foot steel cable by two inches wide with which to pull the logs out of the woods where we had sawed them down. It was necessary to use this long of a cable because of the creek and water through which the logs had to be pulled. It also meant we wouldn't get stuck in the mud with the tractor since we could keep the wheels of the tractor on solid ground to haul the logs out of the woodlot. Following each day's sawing, we loaded the wagon with the sawed lumber and drove it up to the site where Pop had decided the new barn should be built. We stacked the planks and boards in neat piles with space between each row of planks and boards so that they could dry out before being used to build the new barn, It was a wise move on the part of Pop in determining when he thought we had enough lumber sawed and dried before the building of the barn. It actually meant we didn't begin the building of the barn until late in the fall of 1947. Pop had asked his son-in-law, Fritz Schoeck, if he could lay the blocks of the cow barn that he wanted to build. Fritz agreed and came out on two Saturdays to the farm and after Pop had completed the concrete base of the walls, Fritz came out and on two

Saturday mornings completed laying the blocks to the barn walls to a height of twelve feet high. I did the mortar cement mixing for him so that he had plenty of mortar available to lay the concrete blocks on the three sides of the new barn. Pop had already completed putting in the concrete floor to the barn having hired the concrete trucks from Clark's Concrete Company to come out from Syracuse and spread the concrete for the floor and gutters of the new cow barn. The new cow barn walls were superbly set up and formed so that the foundation of the barn seemed to be the professional job of a master mason. The Clark Concrete Trucks dumped the concrete in separate piles from which Pop and I distributed the concrete via our wheel barrows across the floor of this new barn. Pop did all of the masonry work such as setting up the gutters from one end of the barn to the other. He also made sure that the ironwood trees (six inches thick) were properly set and stabilized with concrete holding them in place. We laid the second story boards upon the posts which had been set in the concrete foundation. We then covered the wood with tar paper as a roof that first winter. It was that next spring and summer that we finished the job of building the second story on the hay barn over the new cow barn we had built that previous year. It was then the summer of 1948 that we put all of our bales in the upstairs of the new barn with a width of thirty-six feet by 110 feet length from one end of the new barn from east to west. The last fifty feet were only fifty feet wide. At least we had a barn that not only could house all of the cows and heifers that we had, but all of our machinery as well, including my Jeep, Tractor, wagon, and various tools and machinery which we no longer had to store in the former kitchen of our old farm house! Pop and I had also installed all of the new pipes, hot water tank, and bathtub and showering equipment which Pop and Volkmar had pursued shortly after he, Eva, and David had arrived on the farm in December of 1945 and which they had never taken the time to install because they had so much other work to do in expanding their dairy in order to make more money from which both families could live. Unfortunately, the expansion of the size of the cow barn only took place after Volkmar, Eva and their two boys had moved out and returned to Minnesota.

And Change Finally Came

It was only in my senior year of high school that I could spend full time in high school from the beginning of September until the middle of June. It was also the year my brother, his wife and son, David, came to the farm to begin working on a full time basis with Pop in what both hoped would be a partnership of equals in farming for the years ahead. Unfortunately for both men, this proved to be an impossibility by September of 1946. Volkmar had been promoted to become a Captain in the U. S. Air Force after being transferred from Egypt where he had been posted from 1944 to 1945. Eva, his wife, had been originally agreeable to living on the farm after the war was over. There were no special accommodations such as showers, running water, and a flush toilet in the farm house which had been built in 1793! There was only a chemical toilet in one of the little rooms adjacent to the bedroom of Pop and Mom in the eastern end of the house. The only way access could be gained to this room was through their bedroom. Mom had the job of unloading this toilet on a daily basis plus putting fresh chemicals into the bucket at the bottom of the tank. One way in which Volkmar and Eva could accommodate themselves to this "inconvenience" was to take two urine pots with them each evening so that they wouldn't have to come downstairs and wake everyone up in order to go to the toilet. Fortunately, the house was big enough to have vacant rooms upstairs into which Volkmar and Eva could expand their usage as needed for the storage of clothing, a sleeping room for their son, and urinating as needed throughout the night time without having to awaken anyone else. It should be noted that Volkmar had purchased not only a new pump for the well water, but all of the tubbing and sinks, and shower equipment to be installed as he assumed he and Pop would have time

GROWING UP ON A FARM

to set up after they were living on the farm. Unfortunately, this time never arrived before their second son, Bobby was born in June of 1946! Their summer haying was not completed until after they extended their cow barn and added more cattle to their number of milk cows. By the first of September, Eva gave Volkmar notice

"The boys and I are going back to Minnesota this next weekend. You are welcome to come with us, but we're not going to stay here any longer! You and your father haven't touched the new equipment for the bathroom since it arrived in April! I'm not going to go through the winter without taking a bath anymore!"

And with these words, Volkmar felt he had no choice but to agree. He too, would have to leave the farm and return to Minnesota with Eva and their two sons which they did and Pop and I began to work full time together until September of 1950. I had tried to enter Syracuse University only to be told my grades were not high enough to be admitted to college. Since Syracuse was the only university near by, I couldn't begin to think of trying to enroll in any other college. It would have been simply too expensive. It was then that I worked on the farm during the day and at the Carrier Corporation from 3:30 to 12:00 p.m. each evening. My job didn't begin until I had reached my 18th birthday on December 10, 1946. It was then that I became an employee of the Carrier Corporation on Geddes Street and helped to move their air conditioning equipment to their new plant on Thompson Road. We set up air conditioning units for shipment to different parties in the country and made sure that all of the storage units had the necessary supplies to keep them productive in the new location just to the north of the East Syracuse location. Unfortunately for the employees living in the wider Syracuse area, the Carrier Corporation moved their operations overseas in the late eighties and closed down their company permanently in the United States. I continued working for Carrier Corporation until the middle of March when I quit to help with the farm work full time. It was then that we began cutting down hemlock trees and moved the sawmill down to the woodlot to cut the logs into the necessary building materials for the new barn Pop decided we needed to build in order to expand out dairy operation.

183

An Opportunity to Play Baseball

It was in the spring of 1946 that I finally had an opportunity to play baseball while still in high school. It was on one occasion that we [played Valley High School on our main field behind the combined high school and grade school while the junior team played on the field just behind the school on the field running adjacent to the road heading north over the canal and into the eastern part of Fayetteville. I had been designated as the pitcher of our JV team and was doing rather well in limiting the Vally JV Team to limited hits and only one run. When it was time for our team to be up to bat, two of our team members had already gotten on base with singles when it was my turn to come up to bat. One JV field was located between the back of our school. Since the JV baseball team was built along the road running up the hill to the parking lot just behind our high school, we had a backstop and the layout of the playing field which opened towards the tennis courts which had been built just beyond the outfield behind the third and second bases. The distance was probably more than three hundred fifty feet before the limits of the playing field had been covered. When I came up to bat, I swung at the first pitch from the Valley pitcher and missed. The second pitch was a low ball which I simply watched glide by too low to try to hit. The third pitch seemed to be just right and I swung at it and hit it over the playing field, the tennis courts, and landed in the field just beyond them near the old canal which wandered past the outskirts of the school yard before emptying into the waterway leading into the creek running behind the northern border of the school yard limits. Needless to say, I took time running around the bases since the right an center fielders were having a hard time trying to locate where the ball had landed amid the weeds and burdocks beyond the tennis courts! With this home run we won our game against the Valley JVs and after that I began practicing with the Fayetteville varsity team.

Getting the Cows Each Morning From the Pasture

After Pop and I finished building the new barn, we continued getting up at a quarter to four each morning. Pop got up first and banged on the stove pipe that came up through the room before entering the chimney. I would call out, "Okay. I'm awake."

I got dressed, went downstairs and started up the Jeep to drive up the road to the top of the will. I usually drove along the fence line along the border of our field with the Murray farm just to the east of our fields. The cows were usually somewhere near a clump of trees and as soon as they saw the Jeep coming, they got up and started going towards the roadway leading downhill to the barn. There was always a cow or two that I had to get out of the Jeep to awaken and head her towards the direction the other cows were taking down the road to the cow barn. It proved to be a long line of cows and heifers but eventually they all were headed in the same direction and I simply kept my lights on as they wandered down the road to the cow barn. Pop made sure they were all in the right stanchions and gave them a can full of grain to entice their appetites and begin the process of hooking up the milking machine to the first cows as they came into the barn and into their own stanchions. We then began to milk some of the cows by hand and kept the milking machine moving from cow to cow down the line. By a quarter to seven we were through with the milking and turned the cows out to the barn yard. By seven a. m. we had driven the cows across the road and they were on their way to their pasture fields and the creek to spend the day until we drove them back again and across the road at five o'clock p.m. The milk truck came by at seven-thirty each morning to pick up our milk cans for shipment to the Canastota Milk Plant which shipped the milk to New York City each day.

The Benefit of Baling Hay

One of the big improvements, from my perspective, in processing the way in which we raised each summer, was to have the hay baled each time we had cut it and raked for that purpose. Simply raking the hay into long lines and then making them into hills of hay to be pitched on the wagon was simply too slow a process in getting the hay into the barn before the rain came or we had had enough time in which to bring all of the hay into the barn. It meant I had to contact a number of baler operators to alert them when we were ready to have out hay baled before we could put the bales into the barn. Generally, we had the Naymek brothers do the baling for us since they lived just up the road from us in the neighboring County of Madison on Tacomsa Road. It was much easier to pick up the bales and put them on the hay wagon than to pitch the loose hay on the hay wagon and take each load of loose hay to the barn and have it pulled up by the hay fork and tractor to dump into the hay barn and move the huge bundles of hay into the corners of the hay barn by hay fork to make room for the next load! We could take far more hay on a single load of baled hay then we ever could by having to pitch the loose hay unto the wagon and then pull it up with a hay fork and tractor to deposit it into the hay mow to then be stashed away to make room for the next load of loose hay! It would have been cheaper if we had our own baler, but Pop didn't think he wanted to spend that much money for a machine that would only be used for three months of each year! He felt he was actually saving money by having someone else do the baling for him!

GROWING UP ON A FARM

In retrospect, our farming operation was a very successful operation when Pop and I undertook it together. Not only had we been successful in cutting down the trees to saw them up into building materials for the dew barn that we built, but for the use put to the sawmill which Pop had purchased in 1941 after I bought the new model A John Deere tractor which was strong enough to run the sawmill. The tractors which he and Volkmar had purchased were simply not strong enough to use on the sawmill. Pop and I started cutting down trees in the winters of 1946 and 1947 and it was in March of 1948 that he convinced me to buy the new John Deere model A tractor so that we could use it to run the sawmill. The tractor was just the vehicle that we needed to conduct not only our farming operation, but to use in the wood lot in running the sawmill. The John Deere model BR was useful in the woods to pull the logs out of the sawmill just outside of the woodlot by using a steel cable events to eighty feet long which allowed us to hook up the logs with the cable to pull them through the creek and wet spots in the woods while keeping the tractor safe from getting stuck. The bigger tractor would have had the problem of being too high for the exhaust pipes to be safe from damage that would have been done by the tree branches. The BR was low enough to move under the overhanging limbs and by pulling the eighty foot cable with the logs attached, we had no problem moving these logs out to the sawmill before we sawed them into planks and boards with which to build the new barn.

In building the new barn with the newly sawed lumber, we had more than enough to build the second floor of the barn and roof a distance of 110 feet by thirty feet wide. Not only had Fritz Schoeck built the entire eastern end of the new barn on one Saturday, but it was an excellent example of what a skilled mason could do in a relatively short period of time. He completed the job on a single Saturday! Needless to say, I had to keep up with him in making sure he had enough mortar to complete the job in one day! Pop wanted to pay Fritz for his excellent job, but Fritz refused to accept payment for the work he had done! Unfortunately, for us it meant the rest of the block laying was done by Pop since he did not want to ask Fritz to do the rest of the block laying if he refused to accept any payment! And Pop was not a skilled mason! You could see the result from the way the blocks looked which Pop had laid. Not only were they not cement blocks, but they were made out of a substitute material which looked like cement! He did do a commendable job in building the milk house into the new structure which now housed all of true cows and cattle in one barn. He also made it possible for us to store the tractor and Jeep in this new barn without imposing any limits on how the building could be used.

We not only had plenty of room for our cattle, but for the bales of hay and important equipment which we could keep under cover during the winter. Ii was at this time, however, that I was made aware of the fact that a friend of mine's father had recently died and left money in his will for me to go to college. After discussing this offer with my parents they strongly suggested I accept this opportunity and they would continue to operate the farm as we had for another couple of years. Pop was almost sixty-five and getting to the point where he recognized he couldn't do all of this work by himself much longer. After I told Bob Bolton and his mother that I was thrilled to except this opportunity which Mr. Bolton had offered me and that I would register for admission to Syracuse University for the fall semester of 1950. Pop bought my tractor, my two cows and bought me a Ford coupe to drive back and forth to college. I was all set to change my life's goals from farming to education which ultimately meant receiving three degrees from Syracuse University and one from Boston University and entering the ministry and the field of teaching international politics during the years of my adult life. I then began to write books as I was able to do in my retirement years.

Beginning My Yearly Farming By Dropping Out of High School

In the spring of 1943, I had dropped out of school in order to prepare for the annual spring manure spreading, plowing, and preparing of the fields for spring planting. It was on one of these occasions that Bob Ford, a classmate and neighbor from Mycenae came down late one afternoon for a visit. I was just putting hay into the barn and he caught me out in the field just east of the barn loading the hay wagon from the hillocks which I had made with the tractor and hay rake earlier in the afternoon. As was his habit, Buddy, Volkmar's dog, followed the tractor and wagon out into the field. It was his habit of resting under the hay wagon whenever we were making hay in this nearby field. Bob saw me out in the field and decided to come out and visit while I pitched the hay on the hay wagon. I asked Bob if he had ever driven a John Deere before and he said he hadn't.

"Why don't you get up on the driver's seat and see if you can drive it ahead so that I can keep pitching the hay on the wagon?" I asked him.

"Okay. It's a hand clutch, isn't it?" he asked.

"Yes. All you have to do is push the clutch slowly ahead and the wagon will follow," I told him. He did as I had told him and I noticed the left rear wheel seemed to rise up somewhat. It was then that I noticed Buddy, Volkmar's dog has been lying just ahead of the left rear wheel and when Bob moved the tractor and wagon ahead, he had run right over Buddy's rear hips! As Bob came to a halt, Buddy moved out on his front legs pulling his shattered hind legs and hips

DONALD F. MEGNIN

as he gradually made his way down to the shade trees along the edge of the field. It was obvious he couldn't use his legs anymore. They simply dragged along behind his two front legs as he went down the hill towards the shade of the trees.

"I'm sorry, Fritz. I didn't know he was under the wagon!"

"Well it's not your fault. Bob. It never even occurred to me that he might be lying under the wagon!"

We continued our loading of the hay on the wagon with Bob driving ahead from one pile of hay to another until the wagon was loaded. I then drove the tractor back to the hay barn with Bob standing on the drawbar attaching the wagon to the tractor. Bob apologized again for what happened to Buddy.

"That's okay, Bob. It wasn't your fault. Buddy shouldn't have been lying under the wagon in the first place. I'll have my Dad look him over when he comes home from work. I don't think there's much we can do for him now with his hips completely smashed!"

"Well, I'm sorry. but I didn't know he was even under the wagon before I drove ahead!"

"That's okay, Bob. There's nothing that we can do for him now at any rate. Thanks for your help in driving the tractor."

And with that, Bob Ford drove off on his bicycle to return to his home in Mycenae. When Pop came home I told him what had happened to Buddy and took him out to the lot where Buddy had pulled himself under the shade of the maple trees. Pop looked Buddy over and noticed he really couldn't use his rear legs at all since his hips were smashed from the wagon wheel running over them.

"Es ist zu spät in dem das Buddy überfahren war, Er kann seine hindere Beine nicht mehr benutzen! Hull das Gewehr und shizz em in Kopf. Du kannst ihm dann gleth begraben wo er liegt." ("It's too late to do anything for Buddy now, He can't use his hind legs anymore. Get the rifle and shoot him in the head. You can bury him exactly where he lies.")

And Change Finally Came

It was only in my senior year of high school that I could spend full time in school from the beginning of September unit the middle of June. It was also the year my brother, his wife and son, David, came to the farm to begin working on a full time basis with Pop in what both hoped would be a partnership of equals in farming for the years ahead. Unfortunately, for both men, this proved to be an impossibility by September of 1946. Volkmar had been promoted to become a Captain in the U. S. Air Force after being trans-ferried from Egypt he had been from 1944 to 1945. Eva, his wife, had been living on their farm after the was was over. There were no special accommodations such as showers, running water, and a flush toilet in the farm house which was built in 1793! There was only a chemical toilet in one of the little rooms adjacent to the bedroom of Pop and Mom in the easter end of the house. The only way access could be gained to this room was through their bedroom. Mom had the job of unloading this toilet on a daily basis plus putting fresh chemicals into the bucket at the bottom of the tank. One way in which Volkmar and Eva could accommodate themselves to this "inconvenience" was to take two urine pots with them each evening so that they wouldn't have to come downstairs and wake everyone up in order to go to the toilet. Fortunately, the house was big enough to have vacant rooms upstairs into which Volkmar and Eva could expand their usage as needed for the storage of clothing, a sleeping room for their son, and urinating as needed throughout the night time without having to awaken anyone else. It should be noted that Volkmar had purchased not only a new pump for the well water, but all of the tubbing and sinks, and shower equipment to be installed as he assumed he and Pop would have time to set up after they were living on the farm. Unfortunately, this time never arrived before their second son, Bobby, was born in June of 1946! Their summer haying was not completed until after they extended their cow barn and added more cattle to their number of milk cows. By the first of September, Eva gave Volkmar notice "The boys and I are going back to Minnesota this next weekend. You are welcome to come with us, but we're not going to stay any longer! You and your father haven't touched the equipment of the bathroom since it arrived in April! I'm not going to go through the winter without taking a bath anymore!"

And with these words, Volkmar felt he had no choice but to agree. He too, would have to leave the farm and return to Minnesota with Eva and their two sons which they did and Pop and I began to work full time together until September of 1950. I had tried to enter Syracuse University only to be told my grades from high school were not high enough to be admitted to college! Since Syracuse was the only university near by, I couldn't begin to think of trying to enroll in any other college. It would have been simply too expensive. It was then that I worked on the farm during the day and at the Carrier Corporation from 3:30 to 12:00 p.m. each evening. My job didn't begin until I had reached my 18th birthday on December 10, 1946. It was then that I became an employee of the Carrier Corporation on Geddes Street and helped to move their air conditioning equipment to their new plant on Thompson Road. We set up air conditioning units for shipment to different parts of the country and made sure that all of the storage units had the necessary supplies to keep them productive in their new location just to the north of the East Syracuse location. Unfortunately for the employees living in the wider Syracuse area, the Carrier Corporation moved their operations overseas in the late eighties and closed down their company permanently in the United States. I continued working for Carrier Corporation until the middle of March when I quit

Renting the Old Farm House

After Mom had moved to the house next door to the home where Volkmar, Eva and family lived in Seneca, Pennsylvania, I rented the farm house to a family from Chittenango composed of a mother and her three daughters. With the expectation of renting the house for one hundred seventy-five dollars a month, the family moved in during the fall of that year. After several months in which we had received no rental payment, I wrote the mother a letter indicating that since we had not received any rental payments I was forced to ask them to leave by January 1st. After the deadline arrived, Julie and I drove up to the farm and discovered they had evidently not been living there for a few months. The house was pretty much as it had been left that previous late summer. There was no forwarding address for the family that moved out and the neighbors had no idea where they might have moved. While Julie and I were trying to decide what we should do since we lived in western Pennsylvania, a young man from Mycenae stopped in and talked with us. He wanted to buy the house and rent it to persons who he thought would stop by and use it for overnight trips. We worked out an agreement for him to buy the house plus the lot upon which it stood (200 X 200 feet) for fifteen thousand dollars over a period of five years. He was agreeable to this arrangement and paid us each month. Since he lived in Mycenae where the Daniels family had lived years before, we thought this arrangement would be beneficial both to him and to us. After three months, however, he wrote us a letter indicating he was going to sell the house to a Psychology Professor sine he had accepted another job in Boston repairing houses. Needless tho say, we were left without any alternative except to accept what was now a new reality concerning the house which had been in our family since 1929. The new owner began a project of rebuilding the house on the interior and while he was working on it, I did stop and observe what he was doing to the old house. He was upgrading it and adding rooms on to the rear of the house towards the well and garden. I was really impressed with what he was doing. He then added rooms to the rear of the main house so that it began to resemble what had existed prior to the collapse of the rear of the house due to the winter's snowfall.

Several months later when he had finished his project, I stopped by and told him who I was and asked if I might take a walk through his house since I had grown up in the original house as the youngest son of the owner of the farm.

"No, I don't do that sort of thing," he said. "I'm not interested in having people walk through the house that I've just renovated!"

I almost couldn't believe what I was hearing!

"But I grew up in this house!"

"No. I'm not interested in where you grew up! This is my house and I don't want anyone just walking through it just because they grew up in it!"

And with these words, he shut the door and I had no alternative other than to retreat to my car and return to the hotel where we were staying!

Going Off to College

After I left farming in 1950 to go to college, Pop continued to operate the farm with Mom's help. He continued doing so until 1957 after which he rented out the barn to a man selling building equipment in Chittenango. This man built an office in front of the barn on the north side near the entrance to the barn which Pop had used for years. The salesman stored the lumber in the barn behind which we had always loaded the hay in from the rear side of the barn. There was plenty of room and with the additional space down below in what had been his cow barn, Pop had an enormous amount of space in which to store this salesman's building materials. The business seemed to be doing well. The salesman was selling plenty of building materials with which to build all kinds of buildings including barns and houses. The problem was, Pop was not receiving his monthly pay check for the rental of the barn. After the fifth month, Pop told the renter, "Either you start paying me your monthly rent, or I'm going to have to close down your business!"

"Oh I'll pay you, Fred. I've just not sold as much lumber as I thought I would! I'll start paying with this next month's rent payment after I take out a loan from the local bank."

"All right, but on the first of January, I want you to start paying your monthly rent!"

"Okay. I'll start on January 1st!"

Unfortunately, the barn caught on fire on the first of December from a short in the electrical connection, according to the renter. The fire had broken out at two a.m. and by the time the Chittenango Fire Department arrived, the barn was completely enveloped in flames so that the firemen directed their hoses on watering down the house in order to prevent it from catching fire. Needless to say, thee was nothing left of the barn or its contents by the next morning. The house and the pump house had been spared but the barn and its contents were completely gone.

"I'm sorry, Fred," the Fire Chief said to Pop. "There was really nothing we could do to stop the fire. It had gotten too much headway by the time you called us to come to try to save it."

As a consequence of this fire, the building supply owner claimed, "Since there was nothing the fire department could do to stop the fire, all of the lumber I had stocked in the barn has been completely burned! I'll be lucky if I can even gain some payment for my loss since I wasn't expecting a fire would burn all of my building materials! I was just beginning to take out insurance when the fire happened!"

As a consequence, Pop received nothing for the loss of this barn. He had been fortunate to be able to start his tractor and Jeep and back them out of the barn into the yard before the fire consumed the western end of the barn. As a consequence of this fire, so similar to the fire that consumed all three of his barns on the north side of Route 5 in 1932, he lost everything. He did not carry insurance on the new barn and the renter claimed he didn't have nay insurance on the lumber he had kept in the barn, so that the loss was complete both for the owner and the renter of the barn!

It was only years later, after Pop had died that Mom sold the concrete blocks to builders wishing to take them down and reuse them for the building of homes and barns in Madison County. They paid Mom twenty-five cents per block which they had taken off the foundation of the barn and taken away in their trucks to use in building the homes and barns in the nearby county. Hence, today there is nothing left of this huge barn except for a few blocks and the concrete foundation upon which these blocks had once rested!

My Two Years of Teaching in Thailand

Upon graduating from Syracuse University with a degree in Psychology and International Relations in 1954, I was asked if I would be interested in teaching English to Thai students for two years at Chulalongkorn University in Bangkok, Thailand. I talked it over with my parents and Alex Carmichael as well as the officers of the Syracuse-in-Asia Association and decided I would undertake this assignment for two years. Upon my return from Thailand, I then worked for the DeWitt Community Church as one of their staff members expressly to call on prospective members and as a participant in the Sunday morning services.

By the end of 1957, Pop had given up farming and was helping Mom full time in her baking and bread making ventures.

In the fall of 1957, I enrolled in the Boston University School of Theology as a full-time student. It was there that I first met Julia Mae King from Goshen, Indiana who became my wife in the wedding conducted by Alex Carmichael and Bob Bolton on May 28, 1960 in the Marsh Chapel of Boston University. While a student in my last two years in Seminary, I was an assistant to Dr. Howard Thurman, Dean of Marsh Chapel, and set up a program for children of parents attending the services conducted by Dr. Thurman each Sunday morning. While the parents attended the Sunday morning worship services, I had set up a Sunday School and Service for the children. It was then that I hired Julia Mae King as one of my seven teachers of the children attending each Sunday morning.

Upon graduation from Seminary, we were assigned our first pastorate at the First Ward United Methodist Church at 510 Bear

Street, Syracuse, New York. We stayed there for three years in which time I had completed my Master's Degree in International Relations. I had been given permission by the Church to continue my education while serving as their pastor. I then received a Cokesbury Award to begin graduate work on a doctoral program in International Relations. It was then That I resigned my position as the Pastor of the First Ward United Methodist Church and began my full time study in International Politics.

Upon the completion of my course work in International Relations and Political Science, I received another scholarship from the Shell Foundation to conduct my research for a doctor's degree in International Relations and Politics on German Economic Assistance to India from 1955-'65. Following its completion, I took a job as a Professor of International Relations at Slippery Rock State College in Slippery Rock. Pennsylvania. It became a State University in 1974 where I taught until August, 1994 at which time I retired and began writing books on a variety of subjects. I have now completed twelve of these books.

Removing the Remnants of the Old House

It was a long, cold winter and the snow kept falling day after day. The back part the house hadn't really been used very much since Pop died in 1979. Mom pretty much kept herself in the main part of the house which included the kitchen, bathroom, dinning room, hallway and front bedroom and the upstairs bedrooms. The back part of the had house was relatively locked off from the rest of the house. After a particularly heavy snow fall in February, the back part of the house collapsed in a heap so that she could only exit the house from the front door of the main part of the house. It was on a beautiful day in May when Volkmar and his two sons, David and Bob, came to the farm and began to dismantle the remnants of what remained of the part of the house that had fallen in. Since Volkmar had told us what he was planning to do, Julie and I decided to drive up to the farm from Pennsylvania and help in the cleanup of the collapsed part of the old farm house.

In separating the back section from the main part of the house, we decided to drag the remnants out to the garden and burn the remains since most of the boards had broken and the tar paper from the roofing was beginning to crumble as well. We pulled all of the residue that we could out to the center of the old garden and set it on fire. It burned very well and by the time we had finished tearing the remains apart, it had pretty well already been consumed by the fire. David and Bob did a good job keeping the fire going by feeding it from the mass of boards and roofing which they kept feeding to the fire. By the end of the day, the majority of the debris had been consumed so there was nothing left before dark that evening. In our discussion with Mom, Volk and I suggested it would be a good idea to have a porch built on the rear of the house so that she could sit out there and rest and sleep as she saw fit during the rest of the spring and summer. She thought this was a good idea and hired a local builder from Chittenango to construct the porch for her. By the first of June, the project was finished and Mom had a comfortable place to sit in the sunshine and shade on her back porch during the several summers that she spent there before moving to Pennsylvania for the last years of her life.

How Julie and I Became the Owners

After the deaths of Pop and Mom (Pop in 1979 and Mom in 1989), The three of us (Volkmar, Inge and Donald) decided the value of the farm was around one hundred fifty thousand dollars in this era of the early eighties. We divided all of the property within the house into three units with Volkmar having first choice, Inge the second and I had the third choice. We then for the next pile of goods had Inge as number one, I was number two and Volkmar was number three. We rotated this lineup repeatedly until all of the items had been selected. With respect to the farm, after owning it by the three of us, we talked it over with Volkmar and Inge and they both decided they were not be interested in holding it any longer. Julie and I decided we would buy the farm and equipment which was still left from Volkmar and Inge. They both agreed and after dividing the property into three one-third pieces, as the 1980s came along, Inge asked if we would be interested in buying her share of the farm. Julie and I talked it over and since we had long decided years earlier we wanted to build a house on the hilltop in front of the woods on the south side of the farm, we said we would buy her share of the farm and proceeded to do so over the next few years. after completing our purchase of her share of the farm, Volkmar agreed he probably wouldn't be returning to central New York either and asked if we would be interested in buying his share as well. We agreed and began the process of paying him in big bundles for remaining on the third of the farm which he also still held. By the mid 1980s, we had completed the purchase of the farm from him.

DONALD F. MEGNIN

As I've mentioned, we had thought we had renters for the farm house after it was empty in the 1980s, only to find out it was vacant for several months. After the man who had purchased the Daniels' house in Mycenae came and talked with us about selling the house on a two hundred by two hundred foot lot on Route five in order to develop an overnight guest house for travelers going east and west, he began his monthly payment for three years only to have him sell his investment because he had accepted another job in Boston. The buyer is the current owner, a Professor of Psychology at Syracuse University. We sold one hundred twenty four acres across the road on the north side of Route Five for a housing development to the the Oot Brothers Contractors. We still own sixteen and one quarter acres adjacent to Route Five on the north side of the highway plus the south side hillside, and roadway up the hill, two large fields on the hilltop and five acres of woods on the northern slope of the woods. I should also mention the farmland has been rented to three generations of Durfees who live nearby and are currently milking almost one thousand cows three times a day! What has happened to our farm is the same which has occurred to practically all of the farms that once were located along Route Five in central New York State. While my wife and I are now living in a retirement community in Jamesville, New York. we are in our late eighties. What happens to the rest of the farm that we still own remains to be seen.

And in Conclusion

And thus concludes the early remembrances of the farm from a little boy's perspective including as he reached adult age and had brought his wife to visit the farm for the first days after their marriage in Boston, Massachusetts. While the stories reflect the attempts of a little boy to remember the important experiences of his life on the farm, they may also reflect the gaps and omissions which may have occurred that he no longer remembers. As he approaches ninety, his remembrance skills are beginning to fade. Nevertheless, it has been a pleasure to try to remember what important events had taken place on the Megnin farm, many of which I can still remember! Should I recall some other information which I may have overlooked, I shall try to piece it together for future use should I live that long!

CPSIA information can be obtained
at www.ICGtesting.com
Printed in the USA
BVHW05s0418010818
523214BV00001B/84/P